Germany 1918-1949

Alan White and Eric Hadley

Collins Educational

An imprint of HarperCollins*Publishers*

Acknowledgements

The author and publisher acknowledge the following sources. They have made every effort to trace the copyright holders but where they have failed, they will be happy to make the necessary arrangements at the first opportunity.

We are grateful to the following for permission to reproduce illustrations:

Bilderarchiv Preussischer Kulturbesitz **70**
British Library (Newspaper Library) **9, 13, 17, 25, 28, 43, 50, 91, 96, 99**
British Library **9, 13, 15** (bottom), **17, 25, 28, 43, 50, 91, 96, 99**
British Library of Political and Economic Science **18, 47, 76** (top)
Hulton – Deutsch Collection **5, 15** (top), **24** (top), **26, 29, 32** (top), **36** (top), **39, 60** (bottom), **63, 77**
Imperial War Museum **15** (top), **95**
Internationaal Instituut voor Sociale Geschiedenis **10**
Punch **108**
Solo Syndication and the Centre for the Study of Cartoons and Caricatures, University of Kent **103** (bottom)
Weimar Archive **12, 20, 21, 23, 32** (bottom), **48, 57** (top), **64, 71, 76** (bottom), **83**
Wiener Library **24** (bottom), **36** (bottom), **54, 60** (top), **66** (top and bottom), **69, 73, 80** (top and bottom), **81, 84, 85**

We wish to thank the following who have given permission for the use of copyright material:

Bachman & Turner for extracts from *Weimar Eyewitness* by Egon Larsen, 1976; Chatto & Windus for extracts from *The Berlin Diaries 1940-45* by Marie Vassiltchikov, 1985 and *The Past is Myself* by Christabel Bielenberg; Century Hutchinson for an extract from *Hitler's Mein Kampf* edited by D. C. Watt; T & T Clark for extracts from *The Third Reich and the Christian Churches* by P. Matheson; Collins for extracts from *Diaries and Letters 1930-39* by Harold Nicholson; Columbia University Press for an extract from the *Educational Yearbook of the International Institute of Teachers' Colleges* by I. L. Kandel, 1941; Gilles Cremonesi for extracts from *The Great Inflation* by W. Guttman and P. Meehan, 1975; Duckworth for an extract from *Prelude to Genocide* by Simon Taylor, 1985; Exeter University Press for extracts from *Nazism 1919-45 vols 1 and 2* by J. Noakes and G. Pridham, 1983, 1984; Grafton Books for an extract from *Conversations with Stalin* by M. Djilas, 1962; Jacques Grancher for extracts from *The Order of the SS* by F. Reider, Foulsham, 1981; Harvard University Press for extracts from *Vanguard of Nazism* by R. G. L. Waite, 1952; William Heinemann and Doubleday for an extract from *Decision in Germany* by Lucius Clay, 1950; The Controller of Her Majesty's Stationery Office for extracts from *Documents on British Foreign Policy, Second Series, vols IV, VI and XII;* Monthly Review Foundation for an extract from 'When Biology became Destiny' (© Renate Bridenthal, Atina Grossman and Marion Kaplan) which appeared in the *Monthly Review Press,* 1984; Nelson-Hall for extracts from *Hitler's Third Reich: A Documentary History* by L. L. Snyder; Octagon Books for extracts from *The Nazi State* by W. Ebenstein, 1943; Peter Owen for extracts from *On The Other Side* by M. Wolff-Monckeberg, 1979, translated by Ruth Evans; Oxford University Press for extracts from *Speeches of Adolf Hitler, vol I* by N. Baynes, 1942 and *Documents on Germany Under Occupation* by B. Ruhm von Oppen, 1955, published in conjunction with the Royal Institute of International Affairs; Princeton University Press for an extract from *Matthias Erzberger and the Dilemma of German Democracy* by K. Epstein, 1958; Routledge for an extract from *Propaganda in War 1939-45* by M. Balfour, 1979; Simon & Schuster for extracts from *The Nazi Years: A Documentary History,* ed. by J. Remak; Secker & Warburg for extracts from *The Rise and Fall of the Third Reich* by William L. Shirer and *Strength Through Joy* by H. P. Bleuel, 1973; Weidenfeld & Nicholson for an extract from *Baldwin: a biography* by K. Middlemas and J. Barnes, 1975; University of Michigan Institute of Labour for extracts from *Hitler and His Generals* by H. Deutsch.

Illustrations by David Wilson

Cover picture: Contemporary posters, courtesy of Peter Newark

Collins Educational
An imprint of HarperCollins*Publishers*
77-85 Fulham Palace Road
London W6 8JB

ISBN 0 00 327227 3

Reprinted 1991, 1992, 1993, 1994, 1995 (twice), 1996, 1999

Printed and bound in Great Britain by Scotprint, Musselburgh, Scotland

Contents

Germany Before 1914: Politics, Economy, Society

Key ideas

1. Before 1914 Germany's government was headed by a powerful emperor.
2. Before 1914 Germany's industrial strength was growing rapidly.
3. Relations between the upper class and the working class in Germany before 1914 were poor.

Core skills

1. Knowledge and understanding of the political, economic and social character of Germany before 1914.
2. Empathetic understanding of the attitudes of the different sections of pre-war German society towards each other.

In the mid-19th century there was no one country called Germany. Instead there were nearly 40 separate German-speaking states. The biggest of these was Prussia. A single German Empire was formed only in 1871. Most of the smaller German states did not join this Empire of their own accord but were forced into it by Prussia. Prussia dominated the new Empire. The Prussian King became its Emperor or Kaiser. The Empire was governed by the Kaiser and his ministers. No one else counted for much. There was a parliament or Reichstag elected by all men over the age of 25, but its powers were limited. The Reichstag could approve laws proposed by the Kaiser and his ministers but could not propose laws of its own. More important, the Reichstag had no power to force the Kaiser to remove unpopular ministers or governments.

SOURCE 1 — Edward David, leading Social Democrat, discussing the pre-war REICHSTAG in 1926

The old Reichstag was a sham parliament. It could speak but it really had no say. Members of governments came and went without its co-operation. It had no real means of enforcing its will on the government.

(ed. R. Lutz, 'The Causes of the German Collapse in 1918', Stanford University Press, California, 1934)

SOURCE 2 — Kaiser William II, speaking before 1914

There is only one master in this country. That am I. Who opposes me I shall crush to pieces.

(A. G. Gardiner, 'The War Lords', Dent, 1915)

▶ How democratic a country was Germany before 1914?

In the 50 years before the outbreak of war in 1914 the German Empire emerged as one of the world's industrial giants. Early in the 19th century German industry was backward and undeveloped. After 1850, though, growth was rapid. Germany's chemical and electrical industries became world-beaters. Her coal and steel industries, centred in the Ruhr area, were also formidable. Firms like Thyssen (steel), Krupp (armaments), AEG (electrical) and I. G. Farben (chemicals) were feared and envied by their rivals. It was this industrial base which enabled Germany to fight so effectively when war came.

SOURCE 3 — Germany's industrial progress before 1914

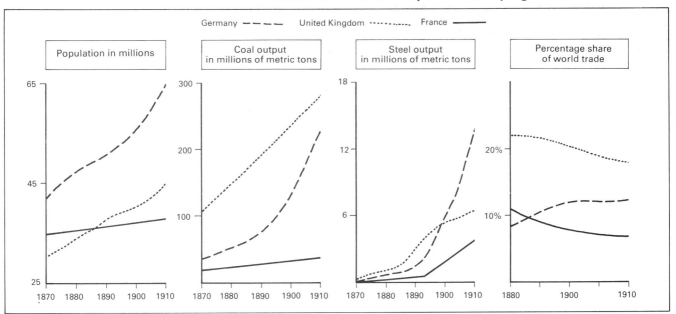

Germany ----   United Kingdom ········   France ———

Population in millions

Coal output in millions of metric tons

Steel output in millions of metric tons

Percentage share of world trade

▶ Is it true to say that as an industrial power Germany had, by 1914,
  i.   left France way behind?
  ii. overtaken Britain?

Kaiser William II

▶ Refer to Source 4. How would you describe the attitude of the German middle class toward the Junkers? Can any conclusions be reached on the basis of this source about the attitude of middle class Germans to the rule of the Kaiser?

German society before the growth of industry was roughly divided into an upper class of landowners, a small middle class of merchants and professional people such as lawyers and doctors, and a lower class of peasants and farm labourers. Industrialisation brought important social changes. A larger and more varied middle class came into being as manufacturers, businessmen and clerical workers grew in number. A new class of industrial workers emerged. These developments led to social tensions.

The most influential group of people in the German Empire was the Prussian landowning class, known as the Junkers. The Junkers held something like a monopoly of key positions in the army and the civil service.

SOURCE 4 — Wendel, a Social Democrat Member of the Reichstag, speaking in 1914

In England the aristocracy has adopted a middle-class outlook. In Germany it is the other way round. The historical development of Germany has resulted in the middle class being moulded by aristocratic and militaristic ideas. The ideal in life for the middle class German is the dashing aristocrat with his upturned moustache. A young businessman in Germany doesn't want to look like a young businessman but if possible like an army officer wearing civilian clothes. A typical middle class youth with ambition first acquires a monocle and then an aristocratic Prussian accent.

(Ebeling and Birkenfeld, 'Die Reise in die Vergangenheit', Georg Westermann Verlag, 1981, authors' translation)

The Junkers' closest allies before 1914 were Germany's leading industrialists. The main enemy of the Junkers and the captains of industry was the working class. The standard of living of German workers in the late 19th century was low. They were as a result attracted to the Social Democratic Party (SPD), founded in 1875, and to its trade unions. The SPD aimed in theory at socialism and revolution but in practice most SPD members were democrats and social reformers. Just before the outbreak of war in 1914 the SPD became the largest single party in the Reichstag, holding nearly one-third of all the seats.

SOURCE 5 — Kaiser William II, speaking in 1889
To me every Social Democrat is an enemy of the realm and of the Fatherland.
(A. G. Gardiner, 'The War Lords', Dent, 1915)

SOURCE 6 — Kaiser William II addressing army recruits, 1891
Recruits! You have sworn loyalty to me; that means, children of my guard, that you have given yourself up to me body and soul. In view of the present socialistic agitations it may come to pass that I shall command you to shoot on your own relatives, brothers, yes, parents — which God forbid — but even then you must follow my command without a murmur.
(A. G. Gardiner, 'The War Lords', Dent, 1915)

SOURCE 7 — New Statesman, British newspaper, 1932
It is difficult for people in England to understand the bitterness of the class struggle in Germany, because they are happily unfamiliar with a tradition which regards the workers as private soldiers, and strikes as mutiny.

▶ Refer to Sources 2, 5, 6 and 7. What was the attitude of the Kaiser and the German upper classes to the SPD?

Questions
1. Explain briefly in your own words the meaning of each of the following terms: Kaiser; Prussia; Reichstag; SPD; Junkers.
2. What reasons did working-class Germans have for opposing the Kaiser's rule?
3. From the point of view of the Kaiser and the Junkers, what were
   i. the advantages and
   ii. the disadvantages of the growth of industry in Germany?

The German Revolution of 1918-1919

Key ideas
1. The First World War led to the Kaiser's downfall.
2. The socialists who controlled Germany after the Kaiser's downfall were divided over the question of how the country should be run.
3. An attempt by left-wing socialists to seize power was put down by the Free Corps.
4. A new constitution for Germany was drawn up at Weimar.

Core skills
1. Knowledge and understanding of the principal events and personalities of the German revolution of 1918-19.
2. Interpretation of a range of primary sources relating to
   i. the divisions among German socialists in 1918-19, and
   ii. the Free Corps.

Rosa Luxemburg

Karl Liebknecht

Friedrich Ebert

When war came Germans buried their differences. The Social Democrats, believing that Germany had to be defended against its enemies, gave their support to the Kaiser. Before long, though, divisions surfaced. Some Social Democrats came to feel that the war was not one of self-defence but was being fought to benefit the ruling classes. In 1917 they broke away from the rest of the Social Democrats and formed a new party to demand peace. It was called the Independent Socialist party. Linked with the Independents at this stage was the small Spartacus League. The Spartacists, named after the leader of a slave rebellion in ancient Rome, were extreme left-wing socialists who believed in seizing power by force. In 1918 they renamed themselves the German Communist party. Their leaders were Rosa Luxemburg and Karl Liebknecht. The Spartacists and the Independents did not, however, win the backing of most Social Democrats. The majority, led by Friedrich Ebert, continued to support the war effort.

Only in late 1918 did the German generals, headed by Ludendorff, give up hope of winning the war. Once they felt defeat was certain they urged the Kaiser to give more power to the politicians of the Reichstag. They did so not because they were democrats but because they wanted the politicians and not the army to get the blame if Germany was treated harshly by the Allies when peace was made. Ebert and other Majority Social Democrats duly joined the government. This move came too late to save the Kaiser. In 1918 Germans were hungry for an end to the war. Support for the anti-war groups, the Independents and the Spartacists, was on the rise. It was widely believed the Kaiser was standing in the way of peace. Calls for him to go began to be heard. Then came the breakdown. Late in October 1918 sailors at the Kiel naval base mutinied after orders had been given for a suicide attack on the British fleet. During the next few days revolt spread across Germany. Control of many cities passed into the hands of hastily-formed workers' and soldiers' councils. In the southern province of Bavaria, Independent Socialists led by Kurt Eisner seized power. At this point the Majority Social Democrats began to fear that Germany could fall apart entirely if the Kaiser stayed.

They announced that they would resign from the government unless he went. On 9 November the Kaiser abdicated and Germany became a republic. A cease-fire or armistice was agreed soon afterwards.

Germany was now under socialist control. The Majority Social Democrats and the Independents patched up their differences and formed a government led by Ebert to look after things while decisions were made about how the country was to be run in future. On this issue, however, there was disagreement.

▶ What do we learn from these sources about
   i. the way in which Independents and Majority Social Democrats disagreed on the issue of Germany's future governments, and
   ii. the reasons for their disagreement?

SOURCE 8 — W. C. Bullitt, American diplomat, writing in late 1918

The Independent Socialists demand that power shall be placed in the hands of the workmens' and soldiers' councils. The Majority Socialists oppose this demand of the Independents and propose that a National Assembly shall be chosen at once by democratic elections to decide the future form of government of the Empire.
('Foreign Relations of the United States, 1919, vol II', American government publication)

SOURCE 9 — Report by an American diplomat of a talk with Otto Cohn, a leading Independent Socialist, 11 December 1918

Dr Cohn said the workmen's and soldiers' councils were potentially democratic organisations, and it was only right that the consolidation of the revolution should be in the hands of those who had always opposed the old regime, not in the hands of those who had actively or passively supported it . . . Dr Cohn asserted that the non-socialist parties had no claim to a seat in the government as they had done nothing to overthrow the Kaiser or the military caste but had remained passive onlookers during the revolution.
('Foreign Relations of the United States, 1919, vol II')

SOURCE 10 — Max Cohen, Majority Social Democrat, speaking in December 1918

The will of the people can only be reflected in a National Assembly elected by every German on an equal footing. The workers' and soldiers' councils can only express the will of some of the people not all of them
(Ebeling and Birkenfeld, 'Die Reise in die Vergangenheit', Georg Westermann Verlag, 1981, authors' translation)

SOURCE 11 — E. L. Dressel, American diplomat, writing early in 1919

The Majority Socialist party leaders are practical common sense men of moderate ideas . . . They see the necessity of working together with members of the new Democratic Party and other moderates in order to stabilise the government.
('Foreign Relations of the United States, 1919, vol II')

The issue of the country's political future was argued out late in 1918 at a meeting of delegates from all of Germany's workers' and soldiers' councils. Since these councils were all under Majority Social Democrat control the result was not in doubt. It was decided that elections for a national assembly would be held in January 1919. The job of this assembly would be to agree upon a new constitution for Germany.

The decision to hold national assembly elections was important because it meant that middle and upper class voters, many of whom hated socialism, would have a big say in deciding how Germany was to be run. Left-wing socialists could see their dream of a truly socialist Germany slipping away. The Spartacists were not prepared to surrender without a fight. A decision was made to try to win control of Germany by means of an armed uprising. Liebknecht and Luxemburg argued against this decision but were outvoted.

The Majority Socialist government — the Independents by this time had left — had no choice but to put down the Spartacist revolt. There was, however, a difficulty. The government was short of troops ready to fight for it. After the armistice the German army had broken up. Ordinary soldiers, sick of war, had simply gone home. The few troops the government did have could not be relied upon to obey orders. The government solved its problem by forming units of armed volunteers. These were the so-called Free Corps. Their organiser was Noske, the minister of defence. The Free Corps were largely made up of men who had been junior officers in the army. Most hated socialism in all its forms. The first thing the Free Corps did was to crush the Spartacists in Berlin. They took Liebknecht and Luxemburg prisoner and murdered them. They then restored order in other parts of Germany. They were at their most brutal when they broke the grip of the revolutionaries in Bavaria. Spartacists who survived called the Majority Social Democrats traitors to the working class for using such men to shoot down former comrades.

SOURCE 12 — 'Liebknecht', a cartoon from Simplicissimus, German magazine, 1919

▶ The top picture of Liebknecht has a caption saying '1917: Spare your enemies'. The caption of the bottom picture is '1919: Murder your brothers'. What criticism does this cartoon make of Liebknecht? Was it a fair criticism?

1917: „Schonet eure Feinde!"

1919: „Mordet eure Brüder!"

9

SOURCE 13 — Von Killinger, Free Corps Commander

The pure Free Corps men did not much care why or for whom they fought. The main thing for them was that they were fighting. War had become their career . . . War made them happy.

(R. G. L. Waite, 'Vanguard of Nazism', Cambridge University Press, 1952)

SOURCE 14 — Facsimiles of Free Corps recruiting posters, 1919

VOLUNTEERS! FLAME THROWER PERSONNEL Enlist in the Flame Thrower Section of THE LUTTEWITZ CORPS Immediate pay plus 5 marks daily bonus FREE FOOD AND EQUIPMENT	*COMRADES* The Spartacus danger has not yet been removed. CAN YOU LOOK ON THIS WITH CALM? NO! Think of what your dead comrades would think! Soldiers, arise! *Prevent Germany from becoming the laughing stock of the earth.* Enrol NOW in THE HUELSON FREE CORPS

▶ What do Sources 13 and 14 tell us about the reasons why men joined the Free Corps? (note: before bonuses, a Free Corps soldier was paid 30-50 marks a week — roughly the wage of an ordinary worker in industry).

SOURCE 15 — Free Corps officer by the artist George Grosz

Prost Noske! — — das Proletariat ist entwaffnet!

▶ The officer is saying 'Cheers, Noske! The young revolution is dead'. How can you tell from this picture that Grosz was an opponent of the Free Corps? How much does this source tell us about the reputation of the Free Corps?

Elections for the national assembly were held soon after the Free Corps had completed their bloody work in Berlin. The Majority Social Democrats failed to win a majority of seats in the new assembly and so formed a coalition government — a government made up of more than one party — with two of the middle-class parties. The assembly met outside Berlin at Weimar because of the unsettled mood in the capital. Within six months it had drawn up a new constitution.

▶ In what way was the Reichstag more powerful under the Weimar constitution than it had been previously?

The Weimar constitution stated that Germany was to be a democracy. The Reichstag or parliament was to make laws and control the government. The government was to be headed by a Chancellor or prime minister. There was also to be a President as head of state. The President was not, however, just a figurehead. Under Article 48 of the constitution he was to have the power in emergencies to rule on his own without the Reichstag.

Inevitably, the new constitution did not win the approval of all Germans. It had enemies on both the political left and the political right. On the left there were communists who wanted a Russian-style government. On the right there were powerful forces which wanted a return to monarchy.

German Revolution timechart

1	OCT 1918:	Majority Social Democrats join government
29	OCT 1918:	Naval mutiny at Kiel
4-8	NOV 1918:	Workers'/soldiers' councils set up throughout Germany
9	NOV 1918:	Abdication of the Kaiser
11	NOV 1918:	Germany agrees to an armistice
16 - 19	NOV 1918:	Berlin conference of delegates from workers'/soldiers' councils
5 - 11	JAN 1919:	Spartacus rising in Berlin
15	JAN 1919:	Free Corps murder Liebknecht and Luxemburg
19	JAN 1919:	National assembly elections
6	FEB 1919:	National assembly meets at Weimar
APRIL-MAY 1919:		Free Corps crush Bavarian revolutionaries
31	JULY 1919:	Assembly approves Weimar constitution

Questions

1. Can we learn anything from Sources 12 and 15 about the social class of
   i. those who supported the Spartacist uprising?
   ii. those who put it down?
2. Mixed up below, on the left are, a number of statements made by prominent Germans in 1918-19 and (on the right) a list of those who made these statements. Work out, using the text and the sources, which speaker made which statement.
   a. 'My purpose was the creation of a force which could restore order in Berlin.'
   b. 'We cannot support the establishment of an elected National Assembly. Authority must lie with the soviets.'
   c. 'The Majority Socialists are the most decent men in Germany.'
   d. 'If I had not used force at this time government would have collapsed.'

   i. Noske, defence minister
   ii. Reinhard, Free Corps commander
   iii. Bullitt, American diplomat
   iv. Daumig, Independent Socialist leader

3. Outline the main events which took place in the province of Bavaria during the German revolution of 1918-19.
4. How would you describe the attitude towards democracy of
   i. Ludendorff
   ii. the Spartacists, and
   iii. Ebert?

11

...ties and Governments in the ...Os

Key ideas
1. In Germany during the 1920s there were several political parties which had a sizeable following.
2. None of these parties was able to win enough support to govern the country on its own.
3. In the 1920s Germany was ruled by a series of unstable coalition governments.

Core skills
1. Knowledge of the main political parties of Weimar Germany and understanding of the differences between them.
2. Analysis of the causes of Germany's political instability in the 1920s.

Alfred Hugenberg

Ernst Thälmann

Germany in the 1920s was a country divided by class and by religion. One result of this was the existence of a variety of political parties. In all, leaving the Nazis aside, there were no less than six major parties.

The GERMAN NATIONALIST PARTY was the party of the landowners and great industrialists who had run Germany before the war. Its members loathed the Weimar Republic and hated socialism. They wanted to restore the monarchy. The Nationalists' leader was the newspaper tycoon Alfred Hugenberg. The GERMAN PEOPLE'S PARTY was a right-wing party like the Nationalists but not so extreme. Its followers would rather have had a monarchy than the Weimar Republic but were not out to destroy the Republic at all costs. The People's Party was a businessman's party. Its leader was Stresemann. The CENTRE PARTY was not as its name suggests a middle-of-the-road party but was the party of Germany's Catholics. It had been founded in 1871 at a time when Catholics were being persecuted by the German government. Its support came from Catholics of all classes — landowners, manufacturers, workers and peasants. Centre Party followers supported the republic and disliked socialism but found it hard to agree on other things. Its leaders in the 1920s included Brüning and von Papen. The DEMOCRATIC PARTY was a middle class party which favoured social reform and opposed any idea of a return to monarchy. Many of Germany's Jews voted for the Democratic Party. Its leading figure until his murder in 1922 was Walter Rathenau. The SOCIAL DEMOCRATIC PARTY was the biggest of the working-class parties. It was a party of social reformers and moderate socialists. It supplied the Weimar Republic with its first President, Ebert. Closely associated with the Social Democrats were most of Germany's biggest trade unions. The GERMAN COMMUNIST PARTY grew out of the Spartacus League. It got a boost in the early 1920s when large numbers of Independent Socialists joined it when their own party fell apart. The Communists competed with the Social Democrats for the votes of the working class. Their leader after 1923 was Ernst Thälmann. The Communists were enemies of the Weimar Republic.

SOURCE 16 — Election results 1919-33

	1919	1920	1924 May	1924 Dec	1928	1930	1932 July	1932 Nov	1933
Communists	-	2	12	9	11	13	14	17	12
Independent Socialists	8	17	1	-	-	-	-	-	-
Social Democratic Party	38	21	21	26	30	24	22	20	19
Democratic Party	19	8	6	6	5	4	1	1	1
Centre Party	20	18	17	18	15	15	16	15	14
German People's Party	4	14	9	10	9	5	1	2	1
German Nationalist Party	10	15	19	21	14	7	6	9	8
Nazis	-	-	7	3	2	18	37	33	44
Minor Parties	1	5	8	7	14	14	3	3	1

▶ The table shows in round numbers the percentage of the total vote won by the main parties in the nine Weimar Republic elections. Would you agree that whoever put the Nazis into power it was not Germany's Catholics or trade unionists? Give reasons for your answer.

Between 1919 and 1933 no party won more than half the votes cast in any election. Because a system of proportional representation was used in the Weimar Republic, this meant that no party got more than half the seats in the Reichstag or parliament. Under proportional representation parties get seats in relation to the percentage of the total vote that they win. A party winning 10% of the vote will get 10% of the seats.

Since none of the parties was able to win a majority of the seats in the Reichstag, none of them was able to govern without help from others. The Weimar Republic was ruled by a series of coalition governments. Forming these coalitions was far from easy. The parties which wanted to overthrow the Republic kept clear of them. The Nazis and Communists never joined coalitions and the Nationalists did so only briefly. Another problem was that parties which did support the Republic could not always agree to work together. The Social Democrats, for instance, were uneasy about co-operating with non-socialists. They did enter coalitions at the beginning and end of the 1920s, but for the most part they left government in the hands of the middle class parties.

SOURCE 17 — Cartoon from Simplicissimus, German magazine, 1920

▶ The caption of this cartoon reads 'Don't push, everyone gets his turn'. The writing over the door says 'Retirement home for government ministers'. What message is the cartoonist trying to put across?

SOURCE 18 — Coalition Governments in the Weimar Republic

▶ Between 1919 and 1930 Germany was run by fourteen different coalition governments. These governments belonged to one of four basic types. Can you explain the names given to the four types of coalition?

▶ How true is it to say that Weimar Germany was run by the middle-class political parties?

Type of coalition	Parties involved					Dates when in office
the Weimar coalition	Social Democrats	Democratic Party	Centre Party			1919-20
the middle class coalition		Democratic Party	Centre Party	People's Party		1920-24 1926
the right wing coalition			Centre Party	People's Party	Nationalist Party	1925 1927-28
the 'big' coalition	Social Democrats	Democratic Party	Centre Party	People's Party		1923 1928-30

Questions

1. Parties which wanted the Weimar Republic to succeed can be described as 'republican': those opposed to it on principle can be called 'anti-republican'. Make lists showing which German parties in the 1920s were 'republican' and which were 'anti-republican'.

2. Which of the following statements about the Social Democratic party are true and which are false? Give a reason for your answer in each case.
   a. The Social Democrats were Germany's most popular party in the 1920s.
   b. The Social Democrats were the most left-wing party in Germany in the 1920s.
   c. The Social Democrats got a lot of support from middle-class voters.
   d. The Social Democrats played little part in the government of Germany during the lifetime of the Weimar Republic.

3. Refer to Source 16. Which parties appear to have lost support to the Nazis after 1930? Were the supporters of these parties before 1930 mostly middle class or working class?

4. Which of the following do you think was the most important cause of Germany's political instability in the 1920s? Give reasons for your answer.
   a. The fact that there were so many political parties.
   b. The fact that political parties found it hard to co-operate.
   c. The system of proportional representation.

The Republic's Problems: The Versailles Treaty

Key ideas
1. Germans objected to the Versailles treaty as a 'dictated peace'.
2. Germans were deeply angered by some of the terms of the Versailles treaty.

Core skills
1. Knowledge and understanding of the terms of the Versailles treaty.
2. Analysis of the causes of German dissatisfaction with the Versailles treaty.
3. Interpretation of a range of primary sources relating to the Versailles treaty.

The armistice of November 1918 stopped the fighting between Germany and her enemies. Technically, though, the two sides were still at war. What was needed to settle things finally was a peace treaty. It was clear enough at the time of the armistice that the terms of peace would be very largely decided by the Allies. They had brought Germany to its knees and were in a position to do much as they liked. In Paris in early 1919 the Allies, headed by the 'Big Three' — Wilson (USA) Lloyd George (Britain) and Clemenceau (France) — spent four months discussing peace terms among themselves. The Germans were then called in and told what was in store.

SOURCE 19 — A facsimile of the front page of the Daily Herald, British newspaper, 8th May 1919

LATE LONDON EDITION

NO. 1,026 (No. 33. - NEW SERIES)   LONDON, THURSDAY, MAY 8, 1919   ONE PENNY

THE PEACE THAT IS NO PEACE

Wholesale Annexation of Territory, Mines and Railways; German Colonies Go to Allies

£1,000,000,000 DEMANDED AT ONCE

Yesterday afternoon the Peace Terms which the Allies have decided to impose upon Germany were presented to the German plenipotentiaries at Versailles.

The Treaty involves sweeping annexations of territory, mines, coalfields, mineral wealth, railways and other valuable property in all parts of the world.

Germany is to lose Alsace-Lorraine, the Saar Valley, Malmedy, Danzig, the greater part of Upper Silesia, Posen, the province of West Prussia on the left bank of the Vistula, and all her Colonies. East Prussia is entirely cut off from the rest of Germany. With a few exceptions, the wishes of the populations concerned are not to be considered.

Germany is to pay £1,000,000,000 at once to the Allies.

Armaments are to be limited and Conscription abolished - in Germany. An attempt is to be made to try the ex-Kaiser. A League of Nations is to be set up. Such is the document which it was intended would "make the world safe for Democracy."

THE MAIN POINTS OF THE TREATY

President Wilson's programme consisted of 14 Points. The draft treaty consists of 13 sections. The main points of the Treaty, a complete summary of which is published on other pages, are as follows:-

LEAGUE OF NATIONS
Section 1 contains the Covenant of the League of Nations. At present it is a League of Allies. Germany is not a member. Nor are her former Allies. Nor is Russia.

ALSACE LORRAINE
Alsace Lorraine goes to France. There is to be no plebiscite.

THE SAAR VALLEY
France receives the coal mines of the Saar Valley. The government is to be in the hands of a Commission of the League of Nations. A plebiscite to be held after 15 years.

LEFT BANK OF THE RHINE
Left Bank of the Rhine and bridgeheads to be occupied by Allies for 15 years. Certain districts may be evacuated after 5 and 10 years. No German fortifications within 50 kilometres east of the Rhine. Germany to pay the cost of the Armies of the Occupation.

SILESIA, POSEN AND WEST PRUSSIA
Germany to cede to Poland the greater part of Upper Silesia, Posen and West Prussia.
Upper Silesia is enormously rich in minerals, especially coal, iron and zinc. It possesses 56 coal mines, employing 90,000 men. Its output of zinc is 208,000 tons - equal to all the rest of Europe put together. Iron founding employs 500,000 men; 54,000 are employed in the textile industry. The loss of Alsace and Lorraine deprives Germany of almost the whole of her supply of iron ore.

DANZIG
Danzig is to be created a Free City under the League of Nations, but within the Polish customs frontiers, and with considerable Polish control. (Danzig is a purely German town. Only 2% of its population is Polish.)

EAST PRUSSIA AND MEMEL
A Plebiscite is to be taken in the southern districts of East Prussia as to whether they should join Poland or remain in Germany, and Memel is to be ceded to the Allies.

SCHLESWIG
A plebiscite is to be taken in Schleswig, the population to decide between German and Danish nationality.

GERMAN COLONIES
Germany to renounce to the Allies all her rights to her overseas possessions.

MILITARY, NAVAL AND AIR CONDITIONS
German army to be reduced to 100,000 men; General staff to be abolished; production of armaments strictly limited - in Germany; no poison gas or tanks to be manufactured - in Germany; Germany prohibited from manufacturing armaments and munitions for foreign countries; no military manoeuvres to be held - in Germany; conscription abolished - in Germany; German fleet limited to 6 battleships, 6 light cruisers, 12 destroyers, 12 torpedo boats; no German submarines; German naval personnel limited to 15,000; Heliogoland to be dismantled; German coast fortifications strictly limited; no military or naval air forces - for Germany.

REPARATION AND RESTITUTION
Germany to make compensation for all damages caused to civilians including pensions; Germany's total obligations to be determined and notified to her not later than May 1, 1921. Payments to be made over 30 years. Germany to pay immediately £1,000,000,000. All German merchant ships of 1,600 tons and over to be ceded to the Allies, and one half of her ships between 1,600 and 1,000 tons, and one quarter of her steam trawlers and fishing boats. Germany to build additonal merchant ships for the Allies during the next four years.

GERMAN AUSTRIA
Germany to recognise entire independence of German Austria. (It has been suggested that German Austria is desirous of becoming united to the German Republic. The French Government is bitterly hostile to such a union, and this clause is possibly an attempt to keep the two branches of the German race apart.)

'The Big Three' — Lloyd George (left), Clemenceau (centre) and Woodrow Wilson (right).

▶ The writer of this article thought that Germany had been treated unfairly by the Allies. Can you detect the reasons why he thought this?

The treaty came as a shattering blow to Germany. The German government's first thought was to refuse to sign it. This, however, would have made little sense. The Allies could have invaded Germany and done as they liked with her if she had refused to sign. The government therefore gave in. Right-wing politicians now attacked those Social Democratic and Centre Party leaders who had agreed to an armistice in the first place. They called them the 'November Criminals'. But it was not only right-wing politicians in Germany who felt bitter at the time the Versailles treaty was signed.

Germany after the Treaty of Versailles

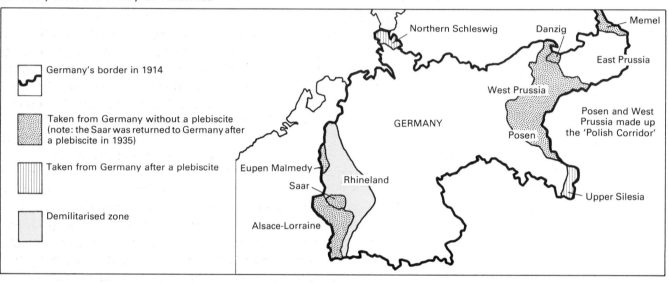

- Germany's border in 1914
- Taken from Germany without a plebiscite (note: the Saar was returned to Germany after a plebiscite in 1935)
- Taken from Germany after a plebiscite
- Demilitarised zone

▶ How widespread in Germany was the resentment caused by the Versailles Treaty?

▶ Which sections of German opinion were most angered by the treaty?

SOURCE 20 — 'How Peace Came To Germany' — A New York Times report, July 1919

The immediate effect of the signing was a blaze of indignation in the Junker press and depression among the people. In Berlin an atmosphere of profound gloom settled on the city. Several papers appeared with black borders on their Versailles articles, beneath such headings as 'Germany's Fate Sealed' and 'Peace with Annihilation'. The right-wing 'Deutsche Zeitung' was suppressed for printing the headline 'Revenge for the Dishonor of 1919' . . . The Evangelical Churches of Germany set aside July 6 as a day of mourning . . . In Berlin on June 24 a number of German officers and soldiers seized 15 flags which had been captured from the French in 1870 and publicly burned them . . . More or less serious mob violence was in evidence, especially in Berlin and Hamburg throughout the week of the signing of the peace.

Germans were outraged by the treaty in part because they felt they had been cheated. The German government thought that it would be invited by the Allies to talks about the peace terms. There were no talks. Germany had to take the treaty or leave it. The Versailles treaty was to Germans a 'Diktat' — a dictated peace. Only in one detail did the Allies change their minds as a result of German protests. Originally they planned to take Upper Silesia away from Germany without a plebiscite — a vote among the local population — but in the end agreed to hold one. There was another reason why Germans felt cheated. This was to do with the 'Fourteen Points', a plan for ending the war which had been put forward by the American President, Wilson, early in 1918.

SOURCE 21 — Cartoon from Simplicissimus, German magazine, July 1919

▶ The caption of this cartoon has the small boy (Woodrow Wilson) saying 'The Tiger has stolen my Fourteen Points'. 'The Tiger' was Clemenceau's nickname. What message do you think the cartoonist is trying to put across?

Germans claimed that their country had agreed to the armistice in the belief that the eventual treaty would be based on the 'Fourteen Points' — only to find that these were ignored by the Allies when they drew up the treaty. In the 'Fourteen Points', for instance, a lot of stress was put on the right of self-determination — the right of people in disputed areas to decide in a plebiscite which country they wished to join. The treaty denied this right to many Germans.

Germans in 1919 were not only bitter because they thought the Allies had cheated them. They also objected very strongly to the contents of the treaty. There was much anger over the losses of land. There were noisy complaints about the loss of the Saar coalfield, even though the treaty made it clear that this was likely to be only a temporary loss. The idea behind the Saar arrangements was to give France a supply of coal while her own mines, destroyed in the war, were repaired. The German view was that France's needs could be met without removing the Saar from Germany's control. The loss of Germany's small overseas empire produced noisier complaints than did the loss of the Saar. The Allies claimed that Germany's colonies had to be taken away because she had shown herself unfit to rule them. This was seen in Germany as a grave insult. The noisiest German complaints, though, arose out of the treatment of Danzig and the so-called 'Polish corridor'. Here Germans were removed from Germany without being given any say in the matter. By contrast, there were few German complaints about the return of Alsace-Lorraine to France. Germany had taken Alsace-Lorraine from France after defeating her in the war of 1871.

SOURCE 22 — Statement by Ebert, Germany's President, May 1919, quoted in The Times
The German people . . . trusted the promise given by the Allies that the peace would be a peace of right on the basis of President Wilson's Fourteen Points. What is now given us in the peace terms is in contradiction of the promise given . . . Such a dictated peace will provoke fresh hatred between the nations and, in the course of history, fresh killing.

▶ What, according to Ebert, was likely to result from a 'Diktat'?

SOURCE 23 — Matthias Erzberger, Government minister, 19 May 1919, quoted in the Daily Herald
As to territorial conditions we cannot assent to the cession of the Saar district, but we are ready in every possible way to guarantee the supply of coal to France till her own mines are restored. Elsewhere, and especially on the Polish frontier, we propose the solution of all disputed questions by a plebiscite.

▶ What do you think the Tageszeitung meant by 'absolute German territory'? Which particular pieces of territory do you think it had in mind?

SOURCE 24 — Tageszeitung, right-wing German newspaper, 8 May 1919, quoted in The Times
What a peace in accordance with French desires looks like is shown by these conditions, which leave nothing of Germany but a torn and tattered territory . . . For Germany there is no self-determination. Absolutely German territory is torn off. This peace is unacceptable.

SOURCE 25 — 'Clemenceau The Vampire': cartoon from Kladderadatsch, German magazine, July 1919

▶ This cartoon, inspired by the loss of the Saar coal mines, shows Clemenceau sucking the blood of 'Germania'. Do you think that it is more or less hostile towards Clemenceau than Source 21?

One of the worst features of the treaty in German eyes was the part of it dealing with the amount Germany was to pay in reparations. The only thing which caused more anger was the treatment of Germans in Danzig and the Polish corridor. The Allies did not in fact fix the precise amount to be paid in reparations until 1921. It was, though, clear enough in 1919 that it was going to be very large indeed. The feeling in Germany was that Allies were out to cripple Germany by demanding more than she could afford.

SOURCE 26 — Reminiscences of Egon Larsen, German journalist

As the terms of peace became known it dawned on us what it meant to lose a war against two dozen nations. The terms were harsh and humiliating; the bill of reparations, to be paid by a Germany shorn of its economic power, was shattering.
(Egon Larsen, 'Weimar Eyewitness', Bachman & Turner, 1976)

Questions

1. Consider the following causes of Germany's anger over the peace terms and, giving reasons, rank them in order of importance: the loss of the colonies; the loss of Alsace-Lorraine; the Saar arrangements; reparations; the treatment of Germans in the Polish corridor; the demilitarisation of the Rhineland.

2. What indications are there in these sources that Germans held France to blame for the treaty's harshness?

3. 'German protests were out of order: the Versailles treaty was fair and reasonable': how far would you agree?

The Republic's Problems: Right-Wing Extremism

Key ideas

1. Right-wing extremists in the early 1920s were nationalistic, anti-socialist and anti-democratic.
2. In 1920 some right-wing extremists took part in the Kapp putsch.
3. After the failure of the Kapp putsch some right-wing extremists began to use murder as a political weapon.

Core skills

1. Knowledge and understanding of the activities of right-wing extremists in Germany in the early 1920s.
2. Analysis of the attitudes and motives of those who took part in the Kapp putsch.
3. Analysis of the motives of members of 'Organisation Consul'.

The early 1920s were a time of violence in Germany. The blame for this lay mainly with right-wing extremists. Men who had fought with the Free Corps in 1919 were involved in many of the worst incidents.

What were the beliefs of these extremist troublemakers? Three things about them are important.

- Right-wing extremists were nationalists. They wanted to see Germany great and powerful. Germany's defeat and the peace treaty left them feeling angry and humiliated.

- Right-wing extremists felt themselves to be Germany's best defence against what they saw as the menace of socialism.

- Right-wing extremists had no time for democracy. They felt that battles for power between political parties divided the nation and weakened it.

SOURCE 27 — Free Corps officer interviewed, 1919

It really turned the stomachs of us old soldiers to see how quickly they got rid of the black-white-red flag of the old Empire. Under this flag thousands of soldiers lie buried in enemy territory. I don't hide the fact I'm a monarchist. When you've served your Emperor for 30 years you can't just say: from tomorrow I'm a republican. Don't worry, though — I don't think we can bring back the monarchy just now.

(authors' translation from a German school textbook)

▶ What was the attitude of Free Corps men towards the Weimar Republic?

In 1920 the Free Corps were involved in a putsch — a bid to seize power by force. What sparked things off was an order by the government disbanding a number of Free Corps units. Before the Versailles treaty the government had planned to build a 400,000 strong army out of the Free Corps. The Versailles treaty limited the army to 100,000 men, so some Free Corps units had to go.

Die Gegenrevolution in Berlin im März 1920
Militär-Propagandaauto
Otto Haeckel, Berlin-Friedenau

The Free Corps Putsch, 1920. The troops are telling Berliners that it isn't their aim to bring back the monarchy.

▶ Why did the Free Corps men accuse Noske of betraying them?

SOURCE 28 — A Free Corps soldier, 1920

Now this minister. This Noske. We had gone through thick and thin with him. He had looked us in the eye and said: 'You are my most loyal men. You came to my help in the darkest hour. You have brought back order to our dear Fatherland. I will never forget it. I will take care of you.' But now he wants to dissolve us and send us out into the streets.

(R. G. L. Waite, 'Vanguard of Nazism', Harvard University Press, 1952)

What happened in 1920 was that Free Corps units refused to obey the government's order to disband. Instead they marched on Berlin. They took control of it with ease. The government fled from the capital. The rebels named Wolfgang Kapp, a little-known politician, as Germany's new leader. Kapp, though, was only a front man. The real leader of the putsch was Luttwitz, a Free Corps commander. The rebels controlled Berlin for only four days. The legal government, which had moved to Stuttgart, called for a general strike. Millions of workers obeyed. It became impossible for the rebels to run the country. They gave up. Few of them received any punishment.

▶ Produce a Free Corps poster of the kind shown in the photograph, explaining why Berlin had been occupied and what sort of Germany the Free Corps hoped to build.

MATTHIAS ERZBERGER * 20·9·1875
DEUTSCHE BUNDESPOST
50

Matthias Erzberger

The Free Corps were broken up after the Kapp putsch. This, however, did not mean that Free Corps men gave up their fight against the Weimar Republic. In 1921 a number of them formed a murder gang called 'Organisation Consul'. Its first major victim was Matthias Erzberger. In 1921 he was shot dead while out walking in the Black Forest. Right-wing extremists were delighted.

Walter Rathenau

▶ Why were Erzberger and Rathenau picked out as targets? What did their murderers hope to achieve by killing them?

▶ What conclusions can be drawn from the figures in Source 30 concerning the political attitudes in the early 1920s of
i. German policemen?
ii. German judges?

SOURCE 29 — Oletzkoer Zeitung, Right-wing newspaper, August 1921

Erzberger had suffered the fate which the vast majority of patriotic Germans have long desired for him. Erzberger, the man who is alone responsible for the humiliating armistice; Erzberger, the man who is responsible for the Versailles 'Treaty of Shame'. Erzberger . . . has at last secured the punishment suitable for a traitor. Regardless of one's feelings about political murder there can be no doubt that the majority of the German people breathe a sigh of relief at this moment.

(quoted in K. Epstein, 'Matthias Erzberger and the Dilemma of German Democracy', Princeton University Press, 1958)

'Organisation Consul' soon struck again. This time its target was Walter Rathenau, one of the ablest politicians in Germany. Rathenau, a Jew, was the country's foreign minister. As foreign minister Rathenau thought that Germany should try to obey the Versailles treaty to the letter. He believed that once the Allies had confidence in Germany they would treat her better. On 24 June 1922 the car in which Rathenau was travelling to work was hit by sub-machine gun fire and a hand grenade. He was killed instantly.

There were hundreds of other political murders in Germany in the early 1920s. Most of them were carried out by right-wing extremists.

SOURCE 30 — Political murders in Germany 1919-23

	MURDERS BY THE EXTREME LEFT	MURDERS BY THE EXTREME RIGHT
Number of murders	22	354
Number of murderers sentenced by the courts	38	24
Average length of prison sentence	15 years	4 months
Number of murderers executed	10	0

Questions

1. Study the extract below from a Social Democrat proclamation of 1920 calling on workers to strike against the Kapp putsch and answer the questions which follow.
'Workers! Party Comrades! The military putsch is here. The Free Corps who were afraid they would be dissolved have made an attempt to overthrow the Republic . . . There is only one way to prevent the return of William II. Paralyse all economic activity!'
   i. What, according to the Social Democrats, were the motives of those who took part in the Kapp putsch?
   ii. Did the Social Democrat proclamation describe the motives of those who took part in the putsch accurately and fully?

2. Do you think that the reputation of Germany's system of government was damaged or improved by the events of 1920?

3. How do you think that a supporter of the Social Democratic party would have reacted to
   i. the statements made in Source 29 and
   ii. the figures contained in Source 30?

The Republic's Problems: The Hyperinflation of 1923

Key ideas
1. In 1923 Germany was the victim of hyperinflation.
2. The hyperinflation of 1923 had a devastating effect on some Germans — but others gained from it.

Core skills
1. Analysis of the causes of the hyperinflation of 1923.
2. Analysis of the consequences of the hyperinflation of 1923.
3. Empathetic understanding of the responses of Germans to hyperinflation.

The word 'inflation' describes a situation in which prices are rising and the value of money is falling. It is commonly said that inflation is caused by too much money chasing too few goods. Inflation occurs, in other words, when the supply of goods fails to keep up with demand. Inflation is not easy to stop once it has got started. An inflationary spiral tends to set in. Rising prices produce a demand for higher wages: higher wages mean that goods cost more to produce: prices have to go up again to pay for the wage increases.

Germany began to suffer serious inflation during the war. The German government did not pay for the war by taxing people more heavily. Instead it paid its bills by printing banknotes. Soon there was too much money chasing too few goods. An inflationary spiral had started.

Things got worse at the end of the war. A huge amount in reparations was demanded from Germany. The sum to be paid was fixed at £6,600,000 in 1921. Many foreigners thought that Germany would be unable to pay. They began to lose confidence in Germany's currency. Foreign banks and businesses expected increasingly large amounts of German money in exchange for their own currency. It became very expensive for Germany to buy food and raw materials from other countries. This led to a further increase in prices in Germany.

▶ There were reasons other than reparations why foreigners lost confidence in Germany's currency in 1919-22. What do you think they were?

Late in 1922 Germany failed to pay an instalment of reparations on time. France replied in January 1923: French troops occupied Germany's main industrial region, the Ruhr. The French were determined to make Germany pay every penny she owed. They wanted to keep Germany weak. A weak Germany meant that France was safe from the threat of attack.

The German government ordered a policy of passive resistance in the Ruhr. Workers were told to do nothing which helped the invaders in any way. What this meant in practice was a general strike. The cost of the government's policy was frightening. All the workers on strike had to be given financial support. The government paid its way by printing more and more banknotes. Germany was soon awash with paper money. The result was hyperinflation.

SOURCE 31 — German poster encouraging passive resistance in the Ruhr, 1923 (the German workman is saying to French troops 'No! You can't force me!')

▶ What else, apart from ordering passive resistance, could the German government have done when France occupied the Ruhr? Why were these other options not taken?

In a hyperinflation era money loses its value extremely quickly. Just how quickly the German mark lost its value in 1923 can be seen in a number of ways:

SOURCE 32 — The price in marks of a loaf of bread in Berlin

December	1918	0.54
December	1921	3.90
December	1922	163.50
January	1923	250.00
March	1923	463.00
June	1923	1,465.00
July	1923	3,465.00
August	1923	69,000.00
September	1923	1,512,000.00
October	1923	1,743,000,000.00
November	1923	201,000,000,000.00

SOURCE 33 — Reminiscences of Egon Larsen, German journalist

You went into a cafe and ordered a cup of coffee at the prices shown on the blackboard over the service hatch: an hour later, when you asked for the bill, it had gone up by a half or even doubled.

(Egon Larsen, 'Weimar Eyewitness', Bachman & Turner, 1976)

SOURCE 34 — Paying wages at a Berlin factory

At eleven o'clock in the morning . . . everybody gathered in the factory forecourt where a five-ton lorry was drawn up loaded brimful with paper money. The chief cashier and his assistants climbed up on top. They read out names and just threw out bundles of notes. As soon as you caught one you made a dash for the nearest shop and just bought anything that was going.

(W. Guttman and P. Meehan, 'The Great Inflation', Saxon House, 1975)

▶ How frequently were people paid when the hyperinflation was at its height?

Children playing with paper money, 1923.

▶ What do you understand by the term 'barter'? Why was an industrial worker going to find it harder than a peasant farmer or a small tradesman to get what he needed through barter?

By late 1923 the paper money issued in Germany had become practically worthless. A banknote with a face value of one hundred thousand million marks was not enough to buy a loaf of bread. The story is told of two women carrying a laundry basket full of paper money through the streets. They put the basket down to look in a shop window. Turning round, they found that the basket had been stolen. The money had been left behind.

Things got so bad in Germany in 1923 that people tried to do without money altogether. They turned instead to barter.

SOURCE 35 — Reminiscences of Egon Larsen, German journalist

Bartering became more and more widespread. Professional people including lawyers accepted food in preference to cash fees. A haircut cost a couple of eggs, and craftsmen such as watchmakers displayed in their shop windows: 'Repairs carried out in exchange for food'. Once I was asked at the box office of our local fleapit cinema if I could bring some coal as the price of two seats.

(Egon Larsen, 'Weimar Eyewitness', Bachman & Turner, 1976)

Hyperinflation was not a disaster for everyone. There were those who did well out of it. People who owed money to others were able to pay off their loans in worthless currency. Big industrialists who had borrowed heavily often profited in this way. Others did well out of hyperinflation by hoarding goods. Foreign visitors to Germany also profited since the value of their own country's currency rose as the value of the German mark fell.

SOURCE 36 — Reminiscences of William Guttman

When I was a student in Freiburg only some 30 miles from the Swiss border there was a regular influx of visitors from nearby Basle. They were quite ordinary people who came for a day's shopping and enjoyment. They filled the best cafes and restaurants, bought luxury goods. Most of us had very little money and could never afford to see the inside of all those glamorous places into which the foreigners crowded. Of course we were envious . . . Contempt for such visitors combined with envy to produce in most of us a great deal of anti-foreigner and nationalist feeling.

(W. Guttman and P. Meehan, 'The Great Inflation', Saxon House, 1975)

Bank notes during the inflation of 1923. (A 'milliard' was one thousand million.)

The biggest losers in 1923 were those with savings. People who had over the years put money into bank accounts or life insurance policies found that hyperinflation had wiped out the value of their savings. The equivalent of five or ten thousand pounds put into a bank in 1914 was worth nothing by late 1923. Most of those who suffered in this way belonged to the middle class. Obviously they were bitter about what happened. For many of them their savings represented a lifetime of hard work.

Papiergeld! Papiergeld!

„Brot! Brot!"

SOURCE 37 — Cartoon from Simplicissimus, German magazine, 1923

▶ The caption of this cartoon has the mother drowning in paper money screaming 'Bread! Bread!' Explain what message the cartoonist was trying to put across.

Working-class Germans did not do too badly in the early stages of the hyperinflation because their unions made sure that their wages went up in line with rising prices. Before long, however, wages began to fall behind prices. Living standards fell. There were serious shortages of food. People went hungry. Children were especially badly affected. In some areas the food shortages threatened to produce a breakdown of law and order.

SOURCE 38 — Report by the Mayor of Berlin, 1923
Countless children, even the youngest, never get a drop of milk and come to school without a warm breakfast . . . The children frequently come to school without a shirt or warm clothing or they are prevented from attending school by a lack of proper clothing. Deprivation gradually stifles any sense of cleanliness and morality and leaves room only for thoughts of the struggle against the hunger and cold.
(F. Schöningh, 'Zeiten und Menschen', 1983, authors' translation)

SOURCE 39 — Evening Standard, British newspaper, 13 October 1923
At Cologne yesterday outbreaks of looting were a frequent occurrence in spite of the activity of all the available police. Many shops remain unopened and others are barricaded . . . Many lorries were held up on their way to market and were looted of potatoes, meat and bread as well as of tobacco and boots.

The 1923 crisis ended when a new government led by Gustav Stresemann came into office in Germany. Stresemann decided to abandon the policy of passive resistance. The Ruhr workers were told to co-operate with the French. Most Germans accepted this decision calmly enough. Right-wing extremists, though, were outraged. They said that a disgraceful surrender had taken place. Once passive resistance was ended, Stresemann was able to tackle the problem of hyperinflation. The old currency was scrapped. A new currency, the Rentenmark, was introduced. The government made it clear that it would not, in future, try to solve its problems by printing paper money. People trusted the new currency. Life returned to something like normal.

Questions
1. How do you suppose hyperinflation affected the attitude of ordinary Germans to
   a. the rich
   b. foreigners
   c. law and order?
2. You are a middle class German who has lost his life savings through hyperinflation. Who do you blame for what has happened to you?
3. Do you suppose the events of 1923 affected the way in which the main sections of German society — upper class, middle class and working class — viewed Germany's system of government? If so, how?

The Republic in the later 20s: Stresemann

Key ideas

1. Stresemann believed that it was in Germany's interest to pursue a foreign policy based on 'fulfilment' of the Versailles peace terms.
2. The policy of 'fulfilment' was detested by extreme right-wingers in Germany.

Core skills

1. Knowledge and understanding of Stresemann's foreign policy.
2. Interpretation and evaluation of primary source material relating to Stresemann's foreign policy.

Gustav Stresemann was the Weimar Republic's most successful politician. He had entered politics before the war as quite an extreme right-winger but by the 1920s he was a moderate. Stresemann was Chancellor for only four months in 1923 but during that time ended passive resistance and brought in the Rentenmark. From late 1923 until his death in 1929 he was foreign minister in coalition governments headed by others.

Stresemann's aim as foreign minister was to restore Germany to something like her old position in Europe. This meant persuading Britain and France to agree to changes in the 1919 peace terms. Stresemann realised that Germany would get nowhere through being awkward. He therefore set out to win the trust of the British and French. He did this by making it clear that Germany would obey the peace terms until changes were agreed. This was known as the policy of 'fulfilment'. It was a successful policy. One thing that helped Stresemann was the attitude of France. The French had been criticised by other countries when they occupied the Ruhr in 1923. After 1923 they adopted a friendlier attitude to Germany.

Stresemann had four major successes as foreign minister.

THE DAWES PLAN, 1924. This made sure that Germany would not have to pay any more than she could afford in reparations each year. Germany's prosperity in the later 1920s owed much to the foreign loans she was able to arrange after the Dawes Plan had gone through.

THE LOCARNO PACT, 1925. At Locarno Germany, France and Belgium agreed to respect the frontiers laid down between them in 1919. What this meant in practice was that Germany gave up any claim to Alsace-Lorraine and Eupen Malmedy while France undertook not to try anything like the Ruhr invasion again.

GERMANY ENTRY INTO THE LEAGUE OF NATIONS, 1926. This showed that Germany was seen as an equal by Britain and France.

THE YOUNG PLAN, 1929. This reduced Germany's reparations bill to less than one-third of the sum fixed in 1921.

Gustav Stresemann

Stresemann's foreign policy was bitterly attacked by right-wing extremists. He was called a traitor. The extreme right was opposed to paying reparations in any form. They said that paying reparations involved admitting the Allies' claim that Germany alone had been responsible for starting the war in 1914. The extreme right particularly disliked the Dawes Plan. This was because it gave the Allies certain rights of control over Germany's railways. Right-wingers said that Germany had been enslaved.

▶ In what ways did Germany at the time of Stresemann's death differ from the Germany of 1923?

SOURCE 40 — Obituary in 'The Times', British newspaper, 4 October 1929

By the death of Herr Stresemann Germany has lost her ablest statesman. Stresemann lived and worked without stint. For the internal reconstruction of his shattered country, as for peace and co-operation abroad, he laboured with magnificent courage and immense energy . . . The task he took up when he became Chancellor would have frightened a smaller man. The French were in the Ruhr, the currency had collapsed, the unsolved problem of reparations hung over an insolvent state seething with popular unrest. Germany seemed to be in ruins, and the man who undertook to give order to the country and to seek a new relation for her with the victors of the war had extremists to right and left determined to obstruct him at every turn . . . The domestic recovery of Germany and her new standing in Europe give the measure of his achievement. Germany is orderly and prospering at home; in the affairs of Europe she has a foremost place; and for these benefits she has to thank the resourceful director of her foreign policy . . . He remained intensely nationalist; but the necessities of Europe led him to the wider nationalism that sees in co-operation the only escape from chaos.

▶ What indications are there in this source of the political sympathies of Vorwärts?

SOURCE 41 — Obituary in 'Vorwärts', German newspaper, 6 October 1929

Stresemann's achievement was in line with the ideas of the international socialist movement. He saw that you can only serve your people by understanding other peoples. To serve collapsed Germany he set out on the path of understanding. He refused to try to get back land which had gone forever. He offered our former enemies friendship. Being a practical man he saw that any other path would have left Germany without any hope of recovery. He covered the long distance from being a nationalist politician of conquest to being a champion of world peace. He fought with great personal courage for the ideals in which he believed . . . It is no wonder that right-wingers watched with horror as he went from his original camp to the opposite one. They could not accept him because doing so involved accepting that the Republic created by the workers had brought Germany from devastation to recovery.

SOURCE 42 — Vorwärts cartoon, 1929

▶ The cartoon has the caption 'Their quarry has escaped them.' The nurse is saying 'You're too late, he (Stresemann) is dead'. The Nazis following Hugenberg are carrying a stink bomb, a bucket of manure and placards saying 'Traitor' and 'Stresemann, rot in hell.' How useful is this cartoon as evidence to someone studying German politics in the 1920s?

Questions

1. Do you think Germany benefited more from the Dawes Plan or the Young Plan?
2. In what ways do Sources 40 and 41 agree about Stresemann?
3. Can you detect any ways in which Sources 40 and 41 disagree about Stresemann?
4. Which do you think gives the fairest and most balanced treatment of Stresemann's achievements — Source 40 or Source 41? Give reasons for your answer.
5. Can you suggest three distinct reasons why right-wing extremists in Germany hated Stresemann?
6. Write a brief obituary of Stresemann from the point of view of a German right-wing extremist.

Hitler and the Origins of Nazism

Key ideas
1. Hitler lived in obscurity for the first thirty years of his life.
2. Hitler's political career began in 1919 when he joined the German Workers Party — soon to be known as the Nazi party.
3. The Nazi programme of 1920 was built around nationalism, anti-semitism and anti-capitalism.

Core skills
1. Knowledge of Hitler's early life.
2. Knowledge and understanding of the ideas put forward by the Nazi party in 1920.

Corporal Hitler, 1916

▶ Using both the information in Source 43 and that in the text, construct a time chart of Hitler's life between 1899 and 1920.

In August 1914 Adolf Hitler stood among a vast crowd in Munich listening to news of Germany's decision to go to war. He was 25 years old, the son of an Austrian customs official. His life before 1914 had been one of failure. He had done poorly at school. He had wanted to train as an artist but in 1907 had failed to win a place at the Vienna Academy of Art. He had then spent several years scratching a living selling pictures, living for most of the time in a Viennese hostel for the destitute — a doss-house.

In 1914, though an Austrian citizen, Hitler joined the German army. He fought on the Western Front throughout the war. He was decorated for bravery, receiving the Iron Cross (Second Class) in December 1914 and the Iron Cross (First Class) — one of the highest awards open to a common soldier — in August 1918.

SOURCE 43 — Hitler's movements, 1889-1920

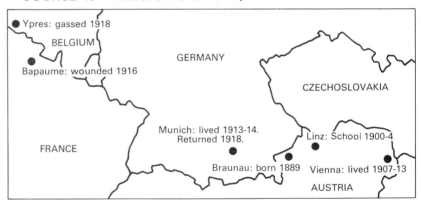

When the war ended Hitler stayed in the army as a member of the Munich garrison's political unit. The unit's main task was to prevent soldiers being influenced by left-wing ideas. One of the jobs Hitler was given involved checking out the so-called German Workers Party. This was a tiny group of right-wing extremists which had been formed in 1918. Its founder was Anton Drexler, a railway worker who wanted to create a nationalist party which appealed to the working classes. Hitler joined Drexler's group in 1919 and soon became one of its leaders. In 1920 he left the army in order to devote himself full-time to building it up.

Not long after Hitler joined the German Workers Party it began to call itself the National Socialist Germany Workers Party. It soon got a nickname — the 'Nazi' party. In 1920 the Nazis put out a 25 point statement of their beliefs. This programme was the work of Hitler and Drexler. Its main ingredients were nationalism, anti-semitism and anti-capitalism.

Nationalism

The Nazi programme called for the creation of a 'Greater Germany' in which all German-speaking peoples were united. It also called for the destruction of the Treaty of Versailles. There was nothing unique in these nationalistic ideas. They were shared by other German right-wing extremists.

Anti-semitism

Someone who is anti-semitic is a hater of Jews. Anti-semitism was widespread in right-wing circles in Germany and Austria in the early 20th century. Hitler seems to have become infected with the idea in Vienna before 1914. By the early 1920s he was making speeches which contained frenzied attacks on Germany's Jews. The Nazi programme of 1920 was openly anti-semitic although it did not employ the violent language which Hitler used in his speeches.

SOURCE 44 — Paul Gierasch, German journalist, writing in the New York Times Current History, November 1923

If Hitler is to be believed, between the German worker and the German employer there would be no conflicts if only Jewish international banking capital were destroyed. Germany would then be freed of all ills and would enter upon a state of order and prosperity.

SOURCE 45 — Points 4 and 5 of the Nazi Programme, 1920

(4) Only members of the nation can be citizens of the state. Only a person of German blood can be a member of the nation. No Jew, therefore can be a member of the nation.

(5) Anyone who is not a citizen of the state may live in Germany only as a guest . . .

(J. Noakes and G. Pridham, 'Nazism 1919-45, vol I', Exeter Uni. Press, 1983)

Closely linked with the Nazis' anti-semitism was their racism. The Nazis claimed that Germans were members of a 'master race' which was superior to all others. Jews were seen as inferior.

SOURCE 46 — Charles Beard, American writer, 1936

According to Nazi doctrine there is such a thing as a pure Aryan race . . . This race has its purest breed in Germany. It must be kept 'pure' . . . Praise for the German race, hatred for Jews, and contempt for other 'inferior and democratic races' — these are the doctrines to be drilled into the minds of Germans.

('Foreign Affairs', April 1936)

▶ How would you argue against Nazi claims that
   i. Jews were a distinct race of people?
   ii. Jews were inferior to 'Aryans'?
   iii. Jews were to blame for all of Germany's problems?

Anti-capitalism

The 1920 Nazi programme was hostile towards the wealthy. It called for an attack on big business in general and on the world of finance in particular. It contained, among other things, demands for the break-up of big businesses and for the confiscation of the wealth of wartime profiteers. These 'socialist' parts of the programme were almost certainly the work of Drexler. Hitler showed little interest in them.

Questions

1. What is the difference between nationalism and racism?
2. Can you give examples of who exactly the Nazis had in mind when they spoke of 'inferior races'? (look at pages 92 and 99 for help).
3. Refer back to Unit 1.5. In what ways were the views of the Nazis the same as those of other right-wing extremists in Germany in the 1920s? In what ways did the views of the Nazis differ from those of other right-wing extremists?
4. Why do you think Hitler and Drexler called their party 'National Socialist'?

The Beer Hall Putsch, 1923

Key ideas

1. In the early 1920s the Nazis believed that they could seize power by force.
2. The Nazis' belief in force led them to create the SA, a private army.
3. A Nazi attempt to seize power by force in 1923 turned into a fiasco.

Core skills

1. Knowledge and understanding of the events of the attempted Nazi putsch in 1923.
2. Analysis of the motives of those involved in the 1923 putsch.

Hitler did not share the leadership of the Nazi party with Drexler and others for long. By 1921 he had made himself the party's undisputed leader. At this time Hitler made no secret of his intention to build up the strength of the party he now controlled by means of force and violence. The Nazis could, of course, have tried to gain power by trying to win Reichstag seats in elections. But Hitler hated elections and democracy. He thought that power in the streets counted for more than seats in the Reichstag.

Hitler's belief in force led in 1921 to the creation of a para-military force or private army. The Nazi private army was called the Sturmabteilung (SA), which means Storm Unit. Because of the colour of their uniforms, SA members quickly became known as Brown Shirts.

SOURCE 47 — Paul Gierasch, anti-Nazi German journalist, writing in 1923

To the Hitler bands flock youths of the featherbrained, unbalanced type, similar to those involved in the Rathenau assassination; students, flotsam and jetsam of the classes that have lost their footing in the new Germany, having been deprived of economic security; clerks, mechanics, even plain hoodlums, such as could once be seen in the following of the Spartacists, purchasable for a few marks, a square meal and the prospect of a free fight with the odds on their side.

('New York Times Current History', November 1923)

▶ What kind of people became members of the SA in the early 1920s?

▶ What were their motives for joining?

By 1923 the membership of the Nazi party had grown to something like 35,000. In spite of its growth it remained a fairly insignificant organisation. The Nazis had no real support in Germany outside the south German state of Bavaria. Inside Bavaria they were only one among many extreme right-wing groups. They were not even the biggest of these groups. They were, however, the most violent.

During 1923 the political situation in Germany developed in ways favourable to the Nazis. The French 'invasion' of the Ruhr and the great inflation between them produced a mood of bitterness. Then Stresemann called off passive resistance. This allowed right-wing extremists to claim that the Weimar Republic and its politicians had betrayed Germany. Hitler was sure the moment had come to march on Berlin and seize power.

The Nazis, though, were not strong enough to act alone. They needed allies. Some of the other extremists in Bavaria were willing to work with them. So too was Ludendorff, the former army chief, who was living in retirement near Munich. Hitler also thought he had the backing of the most powerful men in Bavaria: Kahr, Lossow and Seisser. Kahr headed the Bavarian state government. Lossow was the local army commander. Seisser was Bavaria's police chief. All three men were extreme right-wingers. They told Hitler they would strike when the time was ripe. But they hesitated. Hitler became desperate. He knew that the opportunity offered by the 1923 crisis would not last forever. He had also promised the SA action — and secure jobs in the army after the putsch.

SOURCE 48 — Wilhelm Bruckner, Leader of Munich SA, 1924

I said to Hitler personally: 'The day is coming when I can no longer hold my people. If nothing happens now the men will melt away. We had very many unemployed men among us, men who had spent their last few pence on training, because, as they said, we will strike soon. Then we will be taken into the army and will be out of the entire mess.'

Hitler decided to try and force Kahr and the others to act. On 8 November 1923 Kahr was addressing an evening meeting in one of Munich's beer halls. Lossow and Seisser were also present, Hitler, who had moved SA men into the city, burst into the hall and declared that a putsch was under way. Kahr, Lossow and Seisser were pushed into a side room and forced at gunpoint to agree to take part in the putsch. Hitler, wildly excited, made a speech and then left the beer hall. Foolishly, he allowed Kahr and the others to slip away. They in fact had no intention of joining Hitler. They thought a putsch was bound to fail. Once free, they ordered their forces to move against the Nazis. Hitler, thinking the police and army would be joining him, had made no plans for a fight.

SOURCE 49 — SA men outside the beer hall

Gustav von Kahr, Bavaria's political leader, 1923

▶ Why were SA men putting pressure on their leaders in 1923 to attempt a putsch?

▶ These men were in the middle of an attempt to seize power by force. Do you find anything surprising about their appearance and behaviour?

▶ Can you offer an explanation for their appearance and behaviour?

German stamp (1935) showing SA man and the Feldherrnhalle, where the 1923 killings took place. At the top of the stamp is the slogan 'Remember 9 November 1923!'

Next morning, 9 November, it seemed that Hitler's plan had misfired. But he and Ludendorff decided on one last gamble. Ludendorff had a great reputation in the army. He thought that no soldier would disobey him. So, in a bid to win over the army, Ludendorff and Hitler marched at the head of 3000 SA men on Munich's army headquarters. On the way they met a police barricade. Firing started. Sixteen Nazis were killed. The rest fled. Hitler was arrested a few days later.

Hitler and Ludendorff were put on trial for conspiracy early in 1924. Like other right-wing extremists in the 1920s, they were leniently treated. Ludendorff was found not guilty. Hitler was given a short prison sentence.

The beer hall affair was not so much a Nazi putsch as a Nazi attempt to force others to join them in a putsch. It was a failure. It did, though, provide Hitler with 'heroes' who had died for the cause. He did not allow the Germans to forget them.

Questions

1. Why did German right-wing extremists believe in late 1923 that circumstances were especially favourable for a putsch?
2. 'The men who took part in the Beer Hall putsch in 1923 were of the same type and had the same sort of motives as those who took part in the Kapp putsch in 1920.' Do you agree?
3. 'An attempt to seize control of Bavaria'; 'an attempt to force others into action': which of these do you think best describes Hitler's aim in launching the Beer Hall putsch? Give reasons for your answer.
4. 'In 1923 Hitler behaved in a naïve and simple-minded way'. What arguments can be offered in support of this view?
5. In 1934, after he had come to power, Hitler had Gustav von Kahr murdered. What explanation can you give for this action?
6. Can you suggest reasons why Ludendorff was treated more generously than Hitler at the 1924 trial?

e Nazis in the Later 1920s

Key ideas
1. In prison in 1924 Hitler abandoned the idea of trying to seize power by force and decided to try to gain power by winning seats in elections.
2. The adoption of this new policy did not mean that the Nazis gave up violence altogether.
3. The propaganda of Josef Goebbels was one of the Nazis' main weapons in the fight for votes.

Core skills
1. Knowledge and understanding of Nazi political activities in the later 1920s.
2. Interpretation of a range of primary sources relating to Nazi politics in the later 1920s.

Hitler spent 1924 in prison in the Landsberg fortress outside Munich. In prison he wrote a book describing his early life and his nationalistic, racist and anti-semitic ideas. It was a very long book and a very badly written one. It was published in 1925 under the title 'Mein Kampf' (My Struggle). By 1929 only 20,000 copies had been sold. Things changed after the Nazis came to power in 1933. 'Mein Kampf' then became a best-seller.

The Nazi party fell to pieces while Hitler was in prison. In the absence of strong leadership different groups in the party began to put forward their own ideas about how it should develop. The most important of these was the so-called 'Working Group' led by a young Nazi called Gregor Strasser. Strasser wanted the Nazis to put a lot more emphasis on the anti-capitalist part of their programme. So, when he came out of prison, Hitler faced a challenge to his leadership. He quickly defeated his rival. One of the reasons for Hitler's success was the conduct of another young Nazi, Josef Goebbels. Goebbels started out as one of Strasser's chief supporters. Hitler got him to change sides. He went on to become one of Hitler's most loyal followers.

While in prison Hitler gave a lot of thought to the problem of how to win power. He dismissed the idea of another bid to overthrow the Weimar Republic by force. He was determined not to repeat the mistakes of 1923. He therefore decided upon a policy of 'legality'. This meant that the Nazis would try to win power by contesting elections.

▶ What can be learnt from these sources about the attitudes of Nazi leaders to
 i. democracy
 ii. the Weimar Republic?

SOURCE 50 — Hitler on the Nazis' new tactics, 1923
When I resume active work it will be necessary to pursue a new policy. Instead of working to achieve power by an armed coup, we shall have to hold our noses and enter the Reichstag against the Catholic and Communist members. If out-voting them takes longer than out-shooting them, at least the result will be guaranteed by their own constitution . . . Sooner or later we shall have a majority — and, after that, Germany.
(William L. Shirer, 'The Rise and Fall of the Third Reich', Secker & Warburg, 1960)

SOURCE 51 — Goebbels writing in Der Angriff, 1928
We become members of the Reichstag in order to paralyse Weimar with its own assistance. If democracy is so stupid as to give us salaries for this work, that is its affair. We do not come as friends, nor even as neutrals. We come as enemies. As the wolf bursts into the flock, so we come.

It should not be thought that the Nazis became a law abiding party as a result of their new policy. They in fact gained quite a reputation in the late 1920s for thuggery. Between 1925 and 1930 24 Nazis were killed in street fighting and hundreds were seriously injured. Most of these casualties occurred in clashes with the German Communists and their para-military force, the Red Fighting League. Clashes with the Social Democrats were also common. This violence was not mindless. It was planned and encouraged by Nazi leaders. They welcomed the publicity which violence attracted. They also believed that violence helped to convince middle-class voters that the Nazis were Germany's toughest and most determined anti-communists.

▶ How true do you think it would be to say that in the 1920s the Communists were innocent victims of Nazi attacks?

SOURCE 52 — New Statesman, British newspaper, 27 September 1930, on the 1930 election
The worst enemy the Socialists had to face was the Communists. Between the two parties there was no argument or debate, only hatred and physical violence. In the use of the latter the Communists usually took the offensive. Socialist meetings could hardly be held at all unless there were stalwarts present to throw out Communist hecklers, interrupters, and even raiders armed with sticks and stones. The Nazis, by the way, were the most violent of all. Their attacks (which included beating with sticks, cudgels and knuckle dusters, throwing stones and broken bottles, stabbing and even the occasional use of firearms) were directed against all parties . . . Fights between the Nazis and Communists occurred almost daily.

The Nazis did not, of course, rely on violence alone to get their message across. They also proved to be very adept in the use of propaganda. Propaganda is false or distorted information put out in order to win people's support. Nazi propaganda was spread by means of speeches at party rallies and through the party's various newspapers.

Nazi newspapers in the 1920s

Horst Wessel

The Nazis' most effective propagandist was Josef Goebbels. His most famous exploit during this period involved an SA troop leader named Horst Wessel. In 1930 Wessel was murdered by Ali Hohler, a Communist. The murder seems to have been the result of a private quarrel over the prostitute with whom Wessel lived. No mention of this was made in Goebbels' propaganda. Goebbels endlessly repeated the story that Wessel was a hero who had willingly given up his life for the Nazi cause. A song Wessel had composed became the Nazi marching song. When the Nazis came to power the 'Horst Wessel song' became Germany's second national anthem.

SOURCE 53 — Horst Wessel's grave

The inscription on Horst Wessel's grave, 'Die Fahne Hoch!' ('Raise the flag high!'), is the first line of the Horst Wessel song

▶ This photograph was taken in the 1930s. What indications are there in it of the status which Wessel achieved among Nazis after his death?

Questions

1. Why do you think Hitler decided to give up the idea of trying to win power by force?
2. How much evidence is there in this Unit to support the claim that Hitler showed himself in the later 1920s to be a very skilful political operator?
3. 'Nothing but thugs and hooligans': What evidence is there in the text and in the sources to support this view of the Nazis in the late 1920s?
4. In what ways did Goebbels lie about the circumstances in which Horst Wessel met his death?
5. Refer back to Source 16. How much success did the policy of 'legality' bring the Nazis in the election of 1928?
6. Refer back to Unit 1.7. Why might it be said that the political circumstances of the later 1920s were unfavourable to the Nazis?

Politics 1929-33

Key ideas

1. After 1929 the number of people voting for the Nazi party increased dramatically.
2. In 1930 President Hindenburg was persuaded to make use of the power he had under the Weimar constitution to rule by decree in emergencies.
3. Ambitious individuals — von Schleicher and von Papen — tried to manipulate Hindenburg and to bring the increasingly powerful Nazi party under control, but failed.

Core Skills

1. Analysis of the motives which led many Germans after 1929 to vote for the Nazis.
2. Knowledge and understanding of the political scheming which took place in Germany between 1930 and 1933.

The Nazis' efforts in the late 1920s did not bring them all that much in the way of reward. In the 1928 election they won only 12 out of the 491 seats in the Reichstag. Yet only five years later they were in government. This dramatic rise to power was based largely on a spectacular increase in the number of Germans who were willing to vote for the Nazis. But the increase in the Nazi vote is not the whole story. In order to secure power Hitler had to get past the obstacle of powerful rivals who plotted and schemed against him.

Increases in the Nazi Vote

In 1929 the American economy, the richest in the world, collapsed. Germany's economy was dragged down with it. The sudden withdrawal of American money which had been on loan in Germany made it difficult for German firms to finance their activities. German firms also found that they were unable to sell their goods in the American market. Soon millions of jobs were lost. By 1933 six million Germans were out of work. Those with jobs suffered as well. They had to accept cuts in their wages and standard of living.

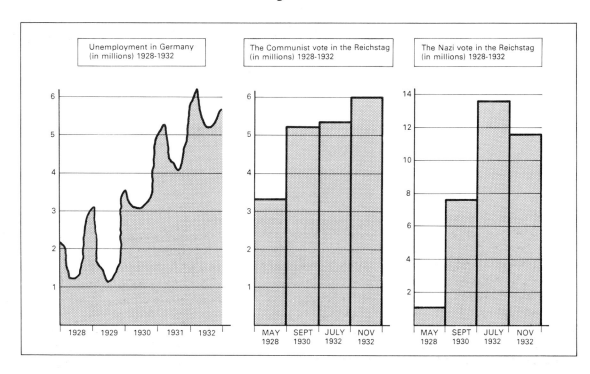

Unemployment in Germany (in millions) 1928-1932

The Communist vote in the Reichstag (in millions) 1928-1932

The Nazi vote in the Reichstag (in millions) 1928-1932

▶ How substantial was the growth in support for the Communist party in Reichstag elections in the early 1930s?

The authorities in Germany were unable to master the economic crisis. They seemed to be helpless in the face of soaring unemployment. The jobless and the poor were therefore attracted to the extreme remedies put forward by the Communists. The Communists began to make gains in national and local elections. This alarmed middle-class Germans. They turned to the Nazis. Previously, respectable middle-class Germans had seen the Nazis as nothing much more than hooligans. Now they saw the Nazis as the best way of preventing the Communists from winning power.

It should not be thought that the Nazis' growing strength in the early 1930s was based on middle-class votes alone. Support for Nazism was not confined to one section of the community. Some working-class Germans were impressed by vague Nazi talk of creating jobs. Many peasant farmers were won over by Nazi promises of a boost for agriculture. Younger Germans seem to have been especially attracted to Nazism.

▶ What can we learn from Sources 54, 55, 56 and 57 about
  i. how, and
  ii. why
the Nazis were able to win the support of many younger German voters?

SOURCE 54 — British Ambassador in Germany, writing in early 1933

Hitler's latest speeches amount to little more than a repetition of his charges against the 'November criminals' and the Marxist government of the last 14 years. These charges are based on such deliberate falsifications of history that one wonders at the credulity of the audience . . . The average National Socialist audience composed very largely of people up to the age of 30 appears to be ignorant of the most elementary historical facts, and when Hitler declares that the revolution of 1918 led to Germany's defeat his audience seem to believe him . . . Hitler may be no statesman, but he is . . . fully alive to every popular instinct. He has convinced the youth of this country that the present unemployment is the work of successive governments of the Left. Germany, he says, is a heap of ruins. The elementary truth is that Germany was a heap of ruins in 1918, and that the German parties of the Left . . . rebuilt it.

(Documents on British Foreign Policy, Second Series, vol IV, HMSO, 1950)

SOURCE 55 — Gregor Strasser, leading Nazi, speaking in early 1933

Strasser admitted that his party did not have a programme, pointing out that in the case of a movement such as that of Hitler, it was the person at the head of the movement who could excite enthusiasm for that movement. A mere programme did not appeal to the masses.

(Documents on British Foreign Policy, Second Series, vol Iv, HMSO, 1950)

SOURCE 56 — Völkischer Beobachter, Nazi newspaper, March 1932

Hitler is the furious will of Germany's youth, which, in the midst of a tired generation, is fighting for new forms, and neither can nor will abandon its faith in a better German future. Hence Hitler is the password and the flaming signal of all who wish for a German future.

(quoted in 'The Nazi Years: A Documentary History', ed. J. Remak, Prentice-Hall Inc.)

SOURCE 57 — New Statesman, British newspaper, Mar(1933
The more one observes here, the more convinced one becomes that the Left has been beaten chiefly on theatrical production. The Weimar Republic has lacked pageantry — uniforms, star performers, torchlight processions. In a contest in these terms, the Nazis knew exactly how to win: they have stormed Germany by procession.

Political Scheming, 1930-33

Paul von Hindenburg, German President, 1925-34

Heinrich Brüning, German Chancellor, 1930-32

In 1930 the moderate parties which governed Germany quarrelled over the issue of how to tackle the country's economic crisis. The government broke up. No new coalition could be formed. The moderates were unable to patch up their quarrel. The extreme parties, the Nazis and the Communists, did not offer to help in the formation of a new coalition. They did not want to keep the Weimar system alive. What they wanted was its destruction. Note, by the way, that the extreme parties were now more important than they had been in the 1920s. After the election of September 1930 they held one-third of the seats in the Reichstag between them.

Germany's economic crisis thus gave rise to a political crisis. The political crisis made the generals who commanded the German army very nervous. They thought that disorder and chaos were not very far away. The generals decided that the situation called for Germany's President to make use of the power he had under Article 48 of the Weimar constitution to rule by decree in emergencies. They therefore set out to persuade the President of the need to act. The chief persuader was Kurt von Schleicher, a smooth, clever, ambitious soldier in his mid-fifties.

Germany's President at this time was Field-Marshal von Hindenburg, a man who had won fame as a wartime army chief. Schleicher found it easy to persuade him to use his emergency powers. Hindenburg had spent his life in the army and was eager to do what it wanted. There was, however, no question of Hindenburg running Germany personally. He was over 80 years old and his mind was no longer sharp. Schleicher's idea was that day-to-day power should be given to a tame politician who would do what the army and the President wanted. The man he had in mind was Heinrich Brüning, an able but colourless member of the Centre Party. In March 1930 Hindenburg duly appointed Brüning Chancellor.

Brüning's appointment as Chancellor brought to an end the 'parliamentary' system which had operated in Germany since 1919. Under this system the right of governments to rule was based on the support they had in the Reichstag. Brüning had little support in the Reichstag. He depended entirely on the President and the army.

For the next two years Brüning ruled by means of emergency decrees signed by Hindenburg. He was not, however, able to turn the economy around. Nor was he able to halt the growth of the extreme parties. This became clear when Hindenburg stood for re-election as President in April 1932. Hitler stood against the

Field-Marshal and did much better than most expected. He won thirteen million votes — double the Nazi total in the 1930 Reichstag elections — to Hindenburg's nineteen million.

At this point Schleicher and the army lost confidence in Brüning. He was dismissed by Hindenburg in May 1932.

The army's next choice as Chancellor was Franz von Papen, a crafty but not very intelligent right-wing nobleman. Outside the army the new Chancellor had very few friends. Only a handful of von Papen supporters were successful when Reichstag elections were held in July 1932. The Nazis, by contrast, did spectacularly well in this election. They became the largest party in the Reichstag.

The Nazis' success made a big impression on Schleicher. He saw that a government backed by the army and by the Nazis could win the kind of popular support that a government backed by the army alone could never have. He therefore set out to draw the Nazis into a partnership with the army.

Schleicher thought that a deal was possible because the army chiefs and the Nazis were both nationalists. There were, however, obstacles in the way of a deal.

▶ What were the obstacles which in 1932 stood in the way of the kind of arrangement between the army and the Nazis which Schleicher wanted?

▶ What do you think Hindenburg meant when he said the Nazis were not 'a reliable national party'?

SOURCE 58 — Hindenburg, speaking in 1931
The Reich President [Hindenburg] referred to . . . the National Socialists who, he feared, were more socialist than nationalist and whose behaviour in the country he could not approve. He . . . had during his East Prussian journey been repeatedly insulted by scandalous demonstrations of National Socialists and had had to comment unfavourably on these young people who had been misled. He did not regard them as a reliable national party.
(J. Noakes and G. Pridham, 'Nazism 1919-45, vol I', Exeter University Press, 1983)

SOURCE 59 — Hindenburg, speaking in August 1932
The President, while having no objection to Hitler on personal grounds, has little confidence in him and does not consider him suitable for the post of Chancellor in view of his very recent naturalisation as a German citizen. He has therefore . . . refused to entertain the idea that Hitler should become Chancellor.
(Documents on British Foreign Policy, Second Series, vol IV, HMSO, 1950)

SOURCE 60 — Hitler and Hindenburg in conversation, August 1932
The President asked Herr Hitler whether he was prepared . . . to enter the Government under the Chancellorship of Herr von Papen. Herr Hitler replied in the negative, and demanded that the President should confer upon him the leadership of the Government, together with entire and complete control in the State.
(Documents on British Foreign Policy, Second Series, vol IV, HMSO, 1950)

Franz von Papen and Kurt von Schleicher

Von Papen called for yet another set of Reichstag elections when the idea of army-Nazi partnership fell through. He hoped that the Nazis would lose support because Hitler had refused to join the government. The gamble failed. In the November 1932 elections the Nazis lost some seats but they remained the Reichstag's largest party. Von Papen now lost Schleicher's confidence. He was dismissed by Hindenburg in December 1932.

Schleicher now came out into the open and became Chancellor himself. He thought he could weaken the Nazis by splitting them. He tried to get Strasser and the more 'socialist' Nazis to break away from Hitler. He failed. He then fell victim to an intrigue by von Papen.

Von Papen was hungry for power. He was bitter about the way he had been treated by Schleicher. He therefore went to the Nazis with the idea of a Hitler-von Papen government. Hitler was interested. His confidence had been dented by the result of the November 1932 election. Von Papen then sold the idea to Hindenburg. Von Papen's main political asset was the fact that the old Field-Marshal had a soft spot for him.

In January 1933 Hindenburg forced Schleicher to resign. He then appointed Hitler Chancellor. Von Papen became Vice-Chancellor. The government they headed was a coalition. There were twelve ministers altogether. Three were Nazis: nine were not.

Questions

1. Construct a time chart of political events in Germany between 1930 and January 1933. Include in your chart Reichstag and presidential elections plus changes in who was Chancellor.
2. Explain in your own words
   i. why many middle class Germans began to vote Nazi after 1929
   ii. why so many young Germans voted Nazi in the early 1930s.
3. Write short paragraphs explaining the part played in German politics in the early 1930s by each of the following: Hindenburg, Bruning, von Papen, Schleicher.

4. 'Democracy came to an end in Germany in 1930.' Write two paragraphs, one arguing in support of this opinion, the other arguing against it.
5. 'There was nothing illegal or unconstitutional about the way Hitler became Chancellor of Germany in 1933'. Would you agree with this view?

e 1933 Election

Key ideas
1. The Nazis' desire to win a clear victory in the 1933 election led to the use of methods of intimidation.
2. The Reichstag fire influenced the outcome of the 1933 election.
3. The Nazis failed to win over half the seats in the 1933 election.

Core skills
1. Analysis of the causes of Nazi success in the 1933 election.
2. Interpretation of a range of primary sources relating to the 1933 election.

In the early 1930s Hitler showed himself to be a skilful political operator. It would have been easy for him during this time to join a government led by somebody else. He did not give in to this temptation. He preferred to wait until he could become Chancellor himself.

Becoming Chancellor, however, did not give Hitler the absolute power he wanted. The government he led was a coalition. Hitler wanted to get rid of his coalition partners so that the Nazis could rule alone. He therefore called for new elections to the Reichstag.

The Nazis' aim in the election was to win more than half the votes cast. Winning over half the votes meant that the Nazis would get more seats in the Reichstag than all other parties put together. Coalition partners would then be unnecessary.

Hitler's main tactic was to try to frighten Germans into voting for him. In his speeches he warned of the danger of a Communist takeover. He said the Nazis needed power in order to stamp out the Communist threat. The message was driven home by Goebbels' propaganda machine.

The election was not a fair fight between the Nazis and their political opponents. The Nazi leaders used every means at their disposal to win. In particular they made use of the power they had as members of the government to give orders and issue decrees.

At the start of the election campaign all Communist meetings were banned and Communist newspapers were shut down. Later on the newspapers of the Social Democrats and the moderate middle-class parties were suppressed.

In Prussia, the state which made up two-thirds of Germany, it soon became clear that banning newspapers was only the beginning. The Nazi Minister of the Interior in Prussia was Hermann Goering.

SOURCE 61 — Goering's order to Prussian policemen, February 1933

Communist terrorist acts and attacks are to be proceeded against with all severity, and weapons must be used ruthlessly when necessary. Police officers who make use of firearms in the execution of their duties will, without regard to the consequence of such use, benefit by my protection; those who, out of a misplaced regard for the consequences, fail in their duty will be punished . . .

(J. Noakes and G. Pridham, 'Nazism 1919-45, vol 1', Exeter University Press, 1983)

▶ A British diplomat said in 1933 that this order could not have been issued in a civilised country. What was so shocking about it?

Goering followed this order by enrolling thousands of Nazis as special constables. SA men were given white arm bands to wear over their brown shirts; they then had all the powers of policemen. In this way Goering deprived the Nazis' opponents of protection against SA attacks. Over fifty anti-Nazis were killed in the weeks before the election. Hundreds more were injured.

The most sensational event of the election campaign came on the night of 27 February, when the Reichstag building in Berlin was burned down. The Nazis claimed that the fire was the work of Marinus van der Lubbe, a Dutch Communist. Many people, however, believed that the Nazis had started it themselves.

SOURCE 62 — Hitler, speaking on the night of 27 February 1933

This is a God-given signal! If this fire, as I believe, turns out to be the work of Communists, there is nothing that shall stop us now crushing out this murder pest with an iron fist.

('Daily Express', 28 February 1933)

SOURCE 63 — Facsimile of a Nazi leaflet

THE REICHSTAG IN FLAMES!

Set alight by Communists!

This is what the whole country would look like if Communism and it ally, Social Democracy come to power!

Innocent citizens shot down as hostages!
Farmers' houses burnt down!

All Germany must join in the outcry:

STAMP OUT COMMUNISM!   SMASH SOCIAL DEMOCRACY!

VOTE FOR HITLER!

▶ Why was the Reichstag fire a highly convenient episode from the Nazi point of view?

▶ What political use did the Nazis make of the fire?

SOURCE 64 — 'Vote for Hitler' (Sunday Express, 5 March 1933)

VOTE FOR HITLER

▶ Britain's ambassador to Germany reported in March 1933 that the Nazis were 'extremely incensed' about foreign press coverage of the election. Why do you think this was?

In the hours following the fire four thousand Communist officials were put under arrest along with a number of other leading anti-Nazis. The next day Hitler persuaded Hindenburg to sign a 'Decree for the Protection of the People and the State'. This decree took away many of the basic rights, such as freedom of speech and assembly, that Germans had under the Weimar constitution. It meant that the Nazis were able to take pretty much what action they liked against their political opponents. In the last few days before the election only the Nazis and their allies, the Nationalists, were able to campaign freely. Voting finally took place on 5 March.

Election results table

	No. of voters (millions) March 1933	No. of voters (millions) Nov. 1932	Seats March 1933	Seats Nov. 1932
COMMUNISTS	4.8	6.0	81	100
SOCIAL DEMOCRATS	7.2	7.2	120	121
CENTRE PARTY	5.5	5.3	92	90
NATIONALISTS	3.1	2.9	52	51
NAZIS	17.3	11.7	288	196
OTHER PARTIES	1.4	1.9	14	26

▶ Do you find anything surprising about these election results?

▶ Do you think the results were a success or a disappointment for the Nazis?

Questions

1. Explain in your own words the contribution made to the outcome of the 1933 election by
   i. the propaganda of Josef Goebbels
   ii. Hermann Goering
   iii. the Reichstag Fire.

2. Explain why the 1933 election campaign did serious damage to the image and reputation of the Nazis outside Germany.

Eliminating the Opposition

Key ideas

1. In 1933 Hitler brought forward an Enabling Bill which made him a dictator.
2. The Enabling Bill was passed by the Reichstag with the support of the Centre party.
3. After the passage of the Enabling Bill Germany became a one-party state.
4. In 1933 powerful institutions in Germany were either destroyed or Nazified.

Core skills

1. Analysis of the motives which led the Centre party to support the Enabling Bill.
2. Knowledge and understanding of the process of 'co-ordination'.
3. Analysis of the motives of non-Nazi Germans for accepting 'co-ordination'.

After the 1933 election the Nazis were in a very strong position in the Reichstag. The Communists who had been elected were unable to take their seats because they were under arrest. Over half of the remaining members were Nazis. The Nazis therefore had more than enough power to carry on the ordinary business of government.

This did not satisfy Hitler. He wanted to be in a position where he could not be obstructed or challenged. This meant crushing those who were against him. Hitler did not, though, want it to be said that he was a gangster who had seized power by force. He wanted to be able to claim that he had a legal basis for his actions.

On 23 March the Nazis presented the Enabling Bill to the Reichstag. It consisted of five short paragraphs. These gave Hitler the power to make laws without the Reichstag. The Enabling Bill, in short, made him a dictator.

The Enabling Bill had to be supported by two-thirds of the Reichstag if it was to become law. This was because the Bill changed the constitution, and constitutional changes required a two-thirds majority. The Bill would not have gone through if the Centre Party — the Catholic party — and the Social Democrats had stood together against it. The Centre Party, however, decided to support the Bill. It was passed by 441 votes to 84.

SOURCE 65 — Speech by Hitler, 23 March 1933
The government regards the Christian churches as important factors in the preservation of our national culture. Their rights will not be infringed. The government guarantee to the churches their due influence in educational matters.
(P. Matheson, 'The Third Reich and the Christian Churches', T. & T. Clark, 1981)

SOURCE 66 — Karl Bachem, Centre Party member
If the Centre had voted against it, it would, given the current mood of the Nazis, probably have been smashed at once . . . All civil servants belonging to the Centre would probably have been dismissed. There would have been a great brawl in the Reichstag, and the Centrists would probably have been beaten up and thrown out. They would have made an heroic exit, but with no benefit to the Catholic cause.
(J. Noakes and G. Pridham, 'Nazism 1919-45, vol 1', Exeter University Press, 1983)

▶ What motives led the Centre Party to vote for the Enabling Bill?

With the Enabling Bill behind them the Nazis quickly went ahead with the process of what they called 'Gleichschaltung' or 'co-ordination'. What this involved was the takeover or the destruction of organisations that stood in their way.

Political parties were among the early victims of 'co-ordination'. The Communists and Social Democrats were outlawed. The Centre and Nationalist parties were pressured into dissolving themselves. Hitler then issued the 'Law Against the Formation of Parties' (July 1933). This declared that the Nazis were the only lawful political party.

The trade unions also fell victim to 'co-ordination'. Germany's biggest trade unions were linked to the Social Democrats. They were powerful organisations. In 1920 they had defeated the Kapp putsch. In May 1933 trade union offices all over Germany were occupied by the Nazis. Trade union leaders were beaten up or arrested. The unions were smashed.

The civil service and the legal profession were not smashed. But they too were 'co-ordinated'. The Nazis took steps to ensure that civil servants and lawyers were loyal to Nazism.

By mid-1933 Hitler had destroyed or taken control of many of the most powerful organisations in Germany. In doing so he had met little really serious opposition.

SOURCE 67 — A Social Democrat resigns from the party, March 1933

As a civil servant I see the tendency on the part of my employer, the state, not to tolerate those belonging to anti-government organisations. I see no other solution but my resignation. The livelihood of my family is at stake.

(J. Noakes and G. Pridham, 'Nazism 1919-45, vol 1', Exeter University Press, 1983)

SOURCE 68 — A report by the British Ambassador, 15 March 1933

During the week which ended on 13 March law and order was practically suspended in most towns . . . Even Dr Brüning himself thought it wiser to change his quarters when he learned that a man resembling him had been attacked in the street . . . It is quite possible that rumours of abductions, floggings and other visitations which have been in circulation here are exaggerated, but that a great deal of injustice has been done is undeniable.

(Documents on British Foreign Policy, Second Series, vol IV, HMSO, 1950)

SOURCE 69 — Karl Bachem on the dissolution of the Centre Party

Younger members of the party are terribly upset and accuse Brüning, Kaas and all the other leaders . . . of cowardice. But what in practical terms could Brüning and Kaas have done? Would it have been of any use to call on the Catholic population to offer united resistance? Such resistance would have at once shown up the physical powerlessness of the party and would have been brutally suppressed . . .

(J. Noakes and G. Pridham, 'Nazism 1919-45, vol 1', Exeter University Press, 1983)

▶ What motives explain the failure of anti-Nazi Germans to put up strong resistance to the process of 'co-ordination'?

SOURCE 70 — 'In these three years I have restored honour and freedom to the German people'
(The Nation, (New York), February 1936)

"In these three years I have restored honor and freedom to the German people!"

▶ How many of the leading Nazis on the platform with Hitler can you identify? (turn to pages 54, 57, 76, 77 and 83 for help).

▶ Can you suggest what organisations other than those mentioned above were 'co-ordinated' and why?

Questions
1. Explain in your own words why Hitler brought forward the Enabling Bill.
2. Explain in your own words why the Nazis embarked on the policy of 'co-ordination'.
3. Why do you think Hitler was not prepared to allow trade unions to operate freely in Germany?
4. Listed below are three courses of action which might have been taken by a Social Democrat in and after 1933. Explain what arguments there were for and against taking each course of action.
    i. Flee abroad and try to weaken Nazism by smuggling anti-Nazi propaganda into Germany.
    ii. Remain in Germany and try to organise an uprising against Nazism.
    iii. Accept that the Nazis had won and do nothing.

The Night of the Long Knives

Key ideas
1. By 1934 Röhm and the SA had become a threat to Hitler.
2. On 30 June 1934 Röhm and other SA leaders were brutally murdered on Hitler's instructions.

Core skills
1. Analysis of the motives which lay behind 'The Night of the Long Knives'.
2. Interpretation of a range of primary sources relating to 'The Night of the Long Knives'.

Ernst Röhm

▶ Would you agree that this article is biased against Röhm and in favour of Hitler? If so, why? (note: the phrase 'perverted debauchery' in Source 71 is a reference to Röhm's homosexuality)

The SA was in the forefront of Nazi activity almost from the beginning. It was SA men who were killed in the 1923 Beer Hall putsch. It was the SA which fought in the street brawls of the later 1920s. In the early 1930s the organisation flourished under a new leader.

SOURCE 71 — 'Story of a Traitor', Daily Express, July 1934
After the great war Röhm came to Hitler as an ex-officer in the Bavarian army. He fought side by side with Hitler during the Munich putsch of 1923. Later when the Storm Troops were restored Röhm became a Storm Troop officer and a Nazi member of the Reichstag. Then, in 1928, he received a call from the Bolivian government to go and reorganise their army and help them fight a war. Röhm, a typical soldier of fortune, left at a loose end by the great war, responded to this call and became a colonel in the Bolivian army. In September 1930 the German elections showed Hitler what an enormous following he was gathering in the Fatherland. He was dissatisfied with Major Pfeffer, the then leader of the Storm Troops. He was looking for a man of the highest military organising ability to replace him. And so he summoned his old comrade Röhm to return from Bolivia. When Röhm took over the Storm Troops they numbered 70,000. Two years later they numbered 500,000 and constituted one of the world's best trained forces of disorder. After the access to power of Hitler, the Storm Troops, flooded with recruits, grew to the monstrous size of four million. The unpopularity of Röhm and his lieutenants, driving round in their expensive motor cars and giving Babylonian banquets, grew greater daily. The working classes contrasted the riotous living of the Brown bosses, who a year ago were nobodies, with their own cut rates of pay and miserable living conditions. Röhm, who made not the slightest secret of his perverted debauchery, became one of the best hated men in Germany. And so Hitler determined to put an end to his existence and that of all his fellow-gangsters, and to make a supreme attempt to crush out gangsterism once and for all in the Nazi machine.

Once Hitler had established himself firmly in power the SA became a threat to him. This was because it began to make demands that he was unable to satisfy. There were three main demands. One was the demand by the SA men for well-paid jobs as a reward for their past services. Next was the demand by leaders of the SA for it to be merged with the German army under Röhm's overall command. Army chiefs were horrified by this idea. Hitler was also against it. He thought that the unruly street fighters of the SA would not make good soldiers. The third demand arose out of the political beliefs of SA leaders. Röhm and his associates were left-wing Nazis. They took the anti-capitalist parts of the Nazi programme seriously. They wanted what they termed a 'second revolution' in which big business would be tamed. Hitler had no intention of attacking the great industrialists. He had never had much sympathy with anti-capitalist Nazis. He was a right-wing Nazi.

At first it seemed that Hitler would try to reach some sort of agreement with the SA leaders. Then he decided that the only way to deal with them was to crush them. In June 1934 he arranged to meet Röhm and other SA leaders at Wiessee, near Munich, in order to discuss the organisation's future. Hitler arrived at Wiessee with a squad of SS men. The SS was a select force which had come into being in 1925 as Hitler's bodyguard. Röhm and dozens of other SA leaders were dragged from their beds by the SS and killed.

▶ What methods did Goebbels use in his broadcast to persuade his listeners that Hitler was to be admired?

SOURCE 72 — Radio broadcast by Goebbels, 1 July 1934
A short council of war and then Hitler's mind is made up. He decides not to wait till the morning but to fly at once to Munich to hunt down the conspirators in their nests. Hitler is determined to seek out personally the nest of conspirators in order to smoke it out ruthlessly. At racing speed we tear off to Wiessee. At seven o'clock we are there. Without the slightest show of resistance we are able to enter the house and surprise a band of conspirators asleep and take them prisoners at once. With unparalleled courage Hitler personally makes the arrests. I do not wish to dwell on the revolting scenes of debauchery which were witnessed by us, but let me quote the words of a simple Hitler guard who declared: 'I only wish the walls could collapse so that the whole nation could witness these happenings and understand how good it is that our leader acts in this way'.
(quoted in the 'Daily Express', 2 July 1934)

It was not only SA leaders who were killed on what became known as the 'Night of the Long Knives'. Hitler also took the opportunity to settle some old scores. The best-known of his victims who were not SA men were General von Schleicher, his predecessor as Chancellor; Gregor Strasser, his rival in the 1920s; and Gustav von Kahr, now aged 73, who had double-crossed him in 1923. Franz von Papen, put under arrest but later released, was lucky to survive.

Opinion in Germany and in the world outside was shocked by the bloodbath of 30 June. Even the Italian dictator Mussolini, no stranger to violence, was staggered by what had happened. Hitler tried to justify what he had done in a major speech to the Reichstag two weeks after the murders.

SOURCE 73 — Hitler's Speech to the Reichstag, 13 July 1934
Without telling me Röhm formed a connection with General von Schleicher. Schleicher it was who gave expression to Röhm's inmost wishes. He put forward the ideas that: *(cont.)*

1. The present regime in Germany could not be continued.
2. The army and navy and all national organisations must be combined in one hand.
3. Röhm was the man for this post.

The preparations made for the revolt were very extensive. Propaganda was circulated among the Storm Troops alleging that the army proposed to dissolve them. It was said that the Storm Troops must forestall this attack . . . I decided to put an end to this impossible development before the blood of thousands had been shed. Therefore I decided to dismiss Röhm and to arrest him and a number of other SA leaders. If disaster was to be prevented I had to act like lightning. Only ruthless and bloody intervention could prevent the revolution from spreading. There was no question then that it was better that a hundred mutineers and conspirators should be destroyed than that 10,000 innocent SA men on the one side and 10,000 innocent men on the other should bleed to death . . . I gave the order to shoot those who were mainly guilty of this treason and I furthermore gave the order to burn out the tumours of our inner poisoning. Everyone will know in future that if he lifts his hand against the state certain death is his fate, and every National Socialist will know that no rank and no position allows him to escape punishment.

(quoted in the 'Daily Herald', 13 July 1934)

▶ What accusation did Hitler make against Röhm and Schleicher in this speech?

▶ Why, according to Hitler, might twenty thousand people have died if he had not moved against Röhm?

▶ What effect did Hitler believe 'The Night of the Long Knives' would have on anyone else thinking of challenging him?

SOURCE 74 — 'Storm Troopers', Daily Herald, 3 July 1934

STORM TROOPERS

(Copyright in all countries.)

▶ What accusation is being made against Hitler in this cartoon?

▶ How fair an accusation was it?

A few weeks after the 'Night of the Long Knives' President Hindenburg died. No new President was appointed. It was announced that the powers of the President were to be transferred to Hitler. The title he gave himself was 'Führer' (leader). Hitler's mastery over Germany was now complete.

Questions

1. Why, according to Source 71, were Röhm and other SA chiefs unpopular in Germany in 1934?
2. Can you think of reasons other than those mentioned in Source 71 why the SA chiefs were widely disliked? (Refer to Units 2.5 and 3.9 for ideas.)
3. Read the extract below from a British newspaper article about the 'Night of the Long Knives' and answer the questions which follow. 'We are still in the dark about the grisly events of June 30. We only know that men whom Hitler praised to the skies are dead. We are told that they are dead because they were engaged in a conspiracy . . . But, so far, not a scrap of evidence has been produced to prove a conspiracy . . .'
   i. In what ways does this article challenge the version of events which Hitler gave to the Reichstag (Source 73)?
   ii. Do the contents of this article prove that Hitler lied when he told the Reichstag that there had been a plot against him? Give reasons for your answer.
4. What evidence is there in Source 71 which suggests that Goebbels could not have been as shocked as he made out (in Source 72) by evidence of Röhm's homosexuality?
5. Do you think that Germany's army chiefs would have been
   i. pleased
   ii. shocked, or
   iii. pleased and shocked by 'The Night of the Long Knives'?
6. What effect do you think that 'The Night of the Long Knives' had on Hitler's reputation outside Germany?

The Nazi Police State

Key ideas

1. Germany became a 'totalitarian' country after 1933.
2. The SS was an important element in Hitler's totalitarian rule.
3. The SS developed from small beginnings into a vast and immensely powerful organisation.

Core skills

1. Knowledge and understanding of the activities of the SS.
2. Analysis of the role of the SS making use of the concepts of continuity and change.

Nazi Germany was a 'totalitarian' country. 'Totalitarian' countries can be thought of as ones which try to establish total control over the lives of their citizens. More particularly, they have each of the following features:

- Only one political party is allowed.
- The ruling party tries to force its ideas on the rest of society and tries to stop people believing in other ideas.
- The ruling party aims to control all aspects of people's lives — there is no area where the citizen is left to think or act as he or she pleases.

Totalitarian countries keep their citizens under constant watch. People who oppose the ruling party are taken out of circulation. In Nazi Germany the tasks of detecting and stamping out opposition were the responsibility of the SS.

The SS was created in 1925. Its full name was the 'Schutzstaffel'. This means 'protection squad'. The purpose for which the SS was formed was to provide Hitler and other Nazi leaders with a bodyguard.

The SS was not a very important organisation in the mid-1920s. It was under the control of the SA and had only a few hundred members.

The SS symbol

Things changed when the SS got a new leader in 1929. This was Heinrich Himmler. Himmler came from a well-off middle-class family. He joined the Nazi party in 1923 after service in the army and the Free Corps. In 1929 he was only 29 years old.

Himmler was ambitious. He aimed to turn the SS into a powerful organisation. It was to be made up of the most fanatical Nazis.

SOURCE 75 — Himmler, speaking in 1937

I decided some time ago, that, if ever I succeeded in uniting in a single organisation a large number of German men of Nordic blood, in making them submit to military obedience . . . then it would be possible to create an élite capable of standing up to any trial.
(F. Reider, 'The Order of the SS,' Foulsham, 1981)

In 1930 the SS and the SA were separated. SS men were given black uniforms to emphasise that they belonged to an independent organisation. The SS continued to provide Hitler with his bodyguard but it was now given an extra task. Hitler made the SS into the Nazi party's internal police force. This involved looking out for members of the Nazi party who were disloyal to Hitler. One of the people Himmler recruited to do this work was Reinhard

Heydrich, a former naval officer. He was soon to become one of the most feared men in Germany.

When the Nazis came to power in 1933 Himmler set out to bring all of Germany's police forces under SS control. There was some opposition to his plans — notably from Goering. Hermann Goering was head of the big state of Prussia and controlled its secret police force, the Gestapo. By 1936, though, Himmler had persuaded Hitler to give him what he wanted.

SOURCE 76 — Britain's Ambassador in Germany, writing in 1934

The fall from grace of the SA has brought about the rise of the SS . . . The SS will probably play an important role in the future. They are individually far superior to the SA . . . What they lack in numbers, they make up for in education, discipline and cold brutality.

(Documents on British Foreign Policy, Second Series, vol XII, HMSO, 1950)

Under the SS Germany's police forces were split into two: the ordinary police and the political police. The political police, which included the Gestapo, was put under the command of Heydrich. Heydrich's forces were able to act outside the law. They could put people into 'protective custody' without a trial. There was nothing the courts could do about this. A country in which the police have power of this kind can be described as a 'police state'.

People taken into 'protective custody' were sent to concentration camps. The first concentration camps had been built to house the Communist and socialists arrested by the Nazis in 1933. Some were run by the SA, others by the SS. The first SS camp was at Dachau. The SS took control of all concentration camps after 'The Night of the Long Knives' in 1934. Special SS squads called 'Death's Head Units' were set up to guard the camps. These units treated prisoners in a barbaric fashion.

SOURCE 77 — The Gestapo Law, 1936

The task of the Gestapo is to investigate and combat all activity throughout Prussia which poses a threat to the state, to collect and assess the results of these investigations . . . Neither the instructions nor the affairs of the Gestapo will be open to review by the courts.

(J. Noakes and G. Pridham, 'Nazism 1919-45, vol 2', Exeter University Press, 1984)

SOURCE 78 — The U.S. Prosecutor, Nuremberg War Crimes Trial, 1946

Since the law was what the Nazis said it was, every form of opposition was rooted out, and every dissenting voice throttled. Germany was in the clutch of a police state, which used the fear of the concentration camp as a means to enforce non-resistance. The Party was the State, the State was the Party, and terror by day and death by night were the policy of both.

(L. L. Snyder, 'Hitler's Third Reich: A Documentary History', Nelson-Hall, Chicago)

The SS reached the height of its power during the war years. It grew into a vast, sprawling empire.

▶ What reason did Hitler have in the mid 1930s for being grateful to the SS?

▶ How did SS men differ from those who had been members of the SA before 1934?

Special SS units called 'Einsatzgruppen' (action squads) were set up to deal with resistance to Nazi rule in German-occupied countries. These units were murder gangs. They went into invaded countries behind the German army and rounded up and killed anyone who was felt to be a threat. In Eastern Europe the 'Einsatzgruppen' were responsible for the deaths of hundreds of thousands of people. Their victims included priests, political leaders and Jews.

In 1941 Hitler made up his mind to wipe out the Jews in areas under Nazi control. The SS was given the task of carrying out this policy of mass murder. Extermination camps like the one at Auschwitz were run by the SS.

Many of Europe's Jews were put to work in SS labour camps before they were put to death. During the war the SS ran huge business enterprises on the basis of slave labour. There were SS-run firms making things like building materials, clothing, furniture and armaments.

In 1940 the SS established an armed force of its own. This was the Waffen (armed) SS. The Waffen SS grew out of Hitler's SS bodyguard. At the start it was a force of no more than a few thousand men. By the end of the war its numbers had risen to more than half a million. The Waffen SS fought alongside the ordinary Germany army. It had a reputation for being ruthless and brutal.

Heinrich Himmler (left) and Reinhard Heydrich

The structure of the SS in the early 1940s.

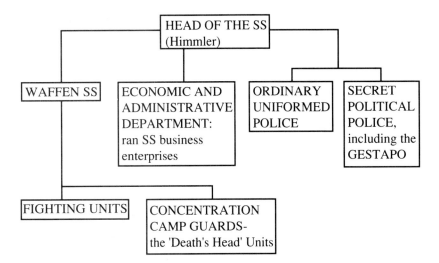

SOURCE 79 — Himmler, speaking in 1943

We have always selected the highest and abandoned the lowest. As long as we maintain this principle, this Order will remain healthy . . . After the war we shall really build up our Order . . . It will be able to fulfil its duty and provide the Germanic people with an élite. This élite . . . will produce the leaders to direct industry, agriculture and politics and the activities of the mind.
(F. Reider, 'The Order of the SS', Foulsham, 1981)

German stamp issued after the murder of Heydrich

Himmler was captured by British troops in 1945 but killed himself before he could be brought to trial. Heydrich was already dead. He had been killed by Czech resistance men in 1942. In retaliation the SS destroyed the Czech village of Lidice and murdered its inhabitants.

Questions

1. Explain how the power of the SS increased in the early 1930s.
2. In what ways did the SS expand and increase its power during the war years?
3. During the war against Russia, Waffen SS units fought with greater savagery and greater determination than units of the regular German army. How would you account for the difference?
4. Look at Sources 75 and 79. What do you think Himmler meant by an 'élite'? What was it about members of the SS whch made them, in Himmler's view, an élite?
5. What characteristics of the SS in its early days in the late 1920s and early 1930s were still present in the much-changed SS of the war years?

The Nazis and the Army

Key ideas
1. During his early years in power Hitler treated the German army well.
2. After 1938 relations between Hitler and the army deteriorated.

Core skills
1. Knowledge and understanding of Hitler's dealings with the German army.
2. Analysis of the causes of changes in the attitudes of German army chiefs towards Hitler.

When Hitler came to power in 1933 he was frightened of the German army. He knew that his government could not survive if the army chiefs ordered their troops into action against it. Hitler therefore made it his business to win the army's support.

> **SOURCE 80 — Hitler, speaking in private, 1934**
> It has always been my view that we can achieve our goals only with the army and never against it.
> (H. Deutsch, 'Hitler and His Generals', University of Minnesota Press)

The army chiefs viewed the Nazi government in 1933 with mixed feelings. Most of them were from upper-class families and so tended to look down on Hitler as a politician risen from the gutter. There were, however, some things that the army chiefs and Hitler had in common. One was nationalism. Another was the belief that Germany needed an army much larger than the force of 100,000 men allowed by the Versailles treaty.

It should be added that the generals did not bear a grudge against Hitler for playing a part in the downfall of von Schleicher's government. The feeling seems to have been that von Schleicher had paid the price for meddling too much in politics.

▶ Why do you think the army escaped 'co-ordination' in 1933?

In 1933 the army escaped the policy of 'co-ordination' applied by the Nazis to other important organisations in Germany. Soon, though, it was involved in a struggle for survival. Ernst Röhm's idea of a merger between the army and the SA was bitterly opposed within the army. The generals knew the army would be swamped by the much larger SA if the idea went ahead. They also believed SA troopers to be little better than hooligans. The army chiefs fought so hard against Röhm's plans that Hitler was forced to choose between the SA and the army. Hitler won their gratitude when he chose to crush the SA in 'The Night of the Long Knives'.

> **SOURCE 81 — The British Consul, Munich, writing in 1934**
> I am informed, upon very good authority, that amongst the officers of the Army there is great optimism, and that it is believed that the Army can now co-operate with the Chancellor in forming a National Socialist State — within reasonable limits — since the SA have been destroyed as a political factor . . . The feeling amongst the Army officers is that Hitler has given the army back its self-respect.
> (Documents on British Foreign Policy, Second Series, vol. 6, HMSO)

Hitler was quick to take advantage of the army's gratitude. A new oath of loyalty was introduced.

▶ Was there any significant difference between the Weimar and Nazi army oaths?

SOURCE 82 — The Weimar Republic Army Oath

I swear to be faithful to the Reich Constitution and vow that, as a brave soldier, I will at all times protect the German Reich and its lawful institutions and will be obedient to the Reich President and to my superiors.

(H. Deutsch, 'Hitler and His Generals', University of Minnesota Press)

SOURCE 83 — The New Army Oath, 1934

I swear by God this sacred oath that I will render unconditional obedience to the Führer of the German Reich and people, Adolf Hitler, the commander-in-chief of the army, and, as a brave soldier, will be prepared at all times to stake my life for this oath.

(H. Deutsch, 'Hitler and His Generals', University of Minnesota Press)

In 1935 Hitler announced that the number of men in the German army was to go up to half a million. This decision — which broke the terms of the Versailles treaty — was welcomed by the army chiefs. A bigger army meant plenty of opportunities for promotion. Support for Hitler within the army reached new heights.

SOURCE 84 — The U.S. Ambassador in Germany, writing in 1936

A firmer basis of mutual respect appears to have developed between the Army and the Party: on the one hand . . . through the Army's realisation of Hitler's usefulness: on the other by virtue of the Party's admiration for the Army as the instrument whose growth has made possible Germany's foreign successes and which is looked to eventually to furnish more.

Field-Marshal von Blomberg

After 1937 relations between Hitler and his generals turned sour. The generals were unenthusiastic when Hitler told them of his plans for a war of conquest in Europe. Hitler decided that they were spineless. Early in 1938 he struck. Field-Marshal von Blomberg, the war minister, was dismissed. He was in no position to resist: the Nazis had discovered that the second wife he had just married had a police record as a prostitute. The commander-in-chief of the army, General von Fritsch, was also forced out: he was falsely accused of having committed homosexual offences. Sixteen other generals were retired and a further 44 were transferred to lesser commands. Hitler had brought the army to heel.

After 1938 Hitler treated the generals with a certain amount of contempt. In 1934 he had promised them that no military force other than the army would be permitted in Germany: he broke his promise when he allowed the Waffen SS to be set up. During the war he took little notice of the expert advice of the generals and was quick to sack them if they failed. Discontent within the army grew. It became very strong after Germany was forced on to the retreat in 1943. In 1944 a number of senior army officers were involved in a plot to kill Hitler. Over two thousand officers were executed when Hitler took his revenge.

General von Fritsch

SOURCE 85 — Field-Marshal von Blomberg, speaking in 1945

Before 1938-9 the German Generals were not opposed to Hitler. There was no reason to oppose him since he produced the results which they desired. After this time some Generals began to condemn his methods and lost confidence in the power of his judgement. However, they failed as a group to take any definite stand against him, although a few of them tried to do so and, as a result, had to pay for this with their lives or their positions.

(Sir J. Wheeler-Bennett, 'The Nemesis of Power: The German Army in Politics', Macmillan, 1953)

▶ Using the text and the sources, decide for each year which word best describes Hitler's relations with the army, and build up a line graph covering the years 1933-44.

	1933	1934	1935	1936	1937	1938	1939	1940	1941	1942	1943	1944
Very good												
Good												
Fair												
Poor												
Very poor												

Questions

1. Would you agree that on balance German army officers welcomed Hitler's arrival in power in 1933? Give reasons for your answer.

2. In 1934 Hitler was forced to choose between the army and the SA. Why do you think he chose the army? (Source 84 will help you to answer this question).

3. Explain in your own words why the German army viewed Hitler
   i.   with enthusiasm in the mid-1930s, and
   ii. with mounting dislike after 1938.

4. Source 85 claims that after 1939 some generals lost confidence in Hitler's power of judgement. Read Unit 4.4 and suggest what decisions made by Hitler during the early years of the war led to this loss of confidence.

The Nazis and the Churches

Key ideas
1. In 1933 Hitler promised the Pope that he would treat German Catholics reasonably but later broke his promise.
2. The Nazis tried to take control of Germany's Protestant churches.
3. Protestants who wanted nothing to do with a Nazi-controlled church set up a 'Confessional Church' of their own.

Core skills
1. Knowledge and understanding of relations between the Nazis and the Christian churches.
2. Analysis of the consequences of Nazi hostility towards Christianity.

In 1933 most Germans were Christian in religion though not all of them, of course, were regular churchgoers. About one-third of the population was Roman Catholic. The other two-thirds belonged to one of the Protestant or 'Evangelical' churches.

Some sort of clash between the Nazis and the Christian churches was inevitable. Nazi beliefs and Christian beliefs were very different. The Nazis knew they would not have total control in Germany until all rival beliefs had been wiped out. They saw no need, though, to rush into conflict with the churches. The churches were also keen to avoid a fight.

SOURCE 86 — William Ebenstein, American writer, 1943
Protestant pastors . . . hated the Weimar Republic because the Catholics and socialists were influential in it . . . In all elections during the Weimar Republic, the Protestant pastors exhorted their followers . . . to vote for those elements, like the Nationalists and Nazis, who desired to bring about the 'national revival' of Germany.
(W. Ebstein, 'The Nazi State', Octagon Books, 1943)

SOURCE 87 — A Catholic conference in Berlin, April 1933
Bishop Föhr reports on the visit of the German ministers to Rome. According to his information Papen and Goering left behind a good impression in the Vatican . . . It is desired that nothing should be done to make the relationship between church and state more difficult. The [Nazi] Movement is valued because of the struggle against Bolshevism and immorality.
(P. Matheson, 'The Third Reich and the Christian Churches', T. & T. Clark, 1981)

▶ Suggest why it was that in 1933 the attitude of
i. the Protestant churches
ii. the Catholic Church
towards Nazism was not altogether unfriendly.

In 1933 Hitler and the Pope reached an agreement about the position of the Catholic church in Germany. Agreements of this kind made by the Pope are called concordats. Hitler wanted a concordat so that he could get rid of the Centre Party without fuss. The Pope wanted to make sure that the church could operate freely in Germany.

In 1933 Hitler promised that the church would be allowed to carry on its religious work without interference. The Pope in return promised that Catholics would stay out of politics. Hitler soon broke his promise. There was interference with church schools and many priests were arrested without good reason. In 1937 Pope Pius XI made his anger known in a famous statement called 'Mit brennender Sorge' (With burning anxiety).

Hitler and the Pope's ambassador to Germany, 1933

After 1937 relations between the Nazis and the Catholic church were bad. Hundreds of priests were put into concentration camps. The Nazis did not, however, launch a full-blooded attack on the church.

The Protestant churches were an easier target for the Nazis than the Catholic church. They were not part of a world-wide organisation. There were also some Protestant ministers who admired Nazism. These were the so-called 'German Christians'. The 'German Christians' wanted to see the Protestant churches under Nazi control. Their leader was Ludwig Müller, an army chaplain.

The Nazis helped the 'German Christians' to become powerful inside the Protestant churches. They made sure that Müller was elected Protestant leader in 1933 and gave him the title of 'Reich Bishop'. Many Protestant clergymen, however, would not accept Müller as their leader. They found the beliefs of the 'German Christians' offensive. One of these beliefs was that Protestant ministers with any Jewish ancestry should be removed from their jobs.

The ministers who would not accept Müller's leadership set up their own organisation. They called it the 'Confessional Church'. The leader of the Confessional Church was Martin Niemöller. Niemöller was famous in Germany. He had been a submarine captain during the first world war. Niemöller and others in the Confessional Church were not frightened to speak out against Nazism.

Martin Niemöller

SOURCE 88 — Statement by the Confessional Church, 1934
We reject the false teaching that the state has the right or the power to exceed its particular responsibility and become sole and total authority in human life thus fulfilling the task of the church as well.
(P. Matheson, 'The Third Reich and the Christian Churches', T. & T. Clark, 1981)

► Which seems to have been the more important cause of Catholic and Protestant criticism of Nazism — Nazi behaviour towards the churches or Nazi behaviour in general?

SOURCE 89 — Statement by the Confessional Church, 1935
There is an official denial of any intention to encroach upon the structure and spiritual life of the Evangelical Church. In fact, however, one encroachment had followed another . . . For a long time now the Evangelical Church has been deprived of its own youth organisations . . . Christian influence and participation in radio, press and public lectures are being pushed more and more into the background . . . The Evangelical conscience is severely burdened by the fact that in Germany concentration camps still exist, and that the measures of the secret state police are still exempt from any judicial investigation.
(P. Matheson, 'The Third Reich and the Christian Churches', T. & T. Clark, 1981)

In the mid-1930s the Nazis cracked down on the Confessional Church. Niemöller was arrested and put into a concentration camp. Hundreds of other Confessional Church ministers suffered a similar fate.

The 'church struggle' did not lead to the destruction of the Christian churches in Germany. Churches remained open. Services were held. But the 'church struggle' did leave the churches in a weakened condition.

SOURCE 90 — Secret report heard at a Protestant conference, 1941
Millions of children grow up in Germany without any religious instruction . . . There is total silence about the church in public. Where does one still see posters advertising church meetings? The newspapers are silent . . . The radio too, is silent . . . The state excludes the church from everything which it considers as belonging to the political sphere . . . There are abrupt confiscations of vast church properties. The fate of the Catholic Church is similar . . .
(P. Matheson, 'The Third Reich and the Christian Churches', T. & T. Clark, 1981)

Questions
1. Write a sentence to explain the meaning of each of the following: concordat; 'German Christians'; the 'Confessional Church'.
2. Why was Martin Niemöller an especially awkward and formidable opponent from the point of view of the Nazis?
3. Which do you think was treated more roughly by the Nazis in the 1930s — the Catholic church or the Protestant churches?
4. Look at Sources 89 and 90. In what ways did the Nazis attack the Christian churches in the 1930s?
5. Would you agree that compared with other organisations the Christian churches came off fairly lightly in their collision with Nazism? Give reasons for your answer.

The Hitler Youth

Key ideas
1. Under the Nazis young Germans were pressured into joining the Hitler Youth movement.
2. The main aims of the Hitler Youth movement were indoctrination and preparation for war.

Core skills
1. Knowledge of the Hitler Youth movement and its activities.
2. Interpretation and evaluation of a range of primary sources relating to the Hitler Youth movement.

Hitler and the Nazis attached a great deal of importance to the young. They knew that it would not be possible to impose Nazi beliefs on the whole of the older generation of Germans. The young were a different matter. The young could, through careful indoctrination, be turned into loyal Nazis. When you indoctrinate someone you get them to believe something so completely that nothing will shake that belief. The indoctrination of young people in Nazi Germany took place in the schools and, outside school hours, in the Hitler Youth.

The Hitler Youth movement was established before the Nazis came into power. It began life as the SA's youth section. In 1933 it had about 100,000 members.

In 1933 the Nazis closed down youth organisations connected with other political parties. Youth organisations linked with the churches were dissolved later on. The Hitler Youth, with no competition, grew rapidly. By 1936 it had four million members. In 1936 the Hitler Youth Law was passed. This made membership of the Hitler Youth to all intents and purposes compulsory. It was possible, however, to pay the required subscription and avoid taking an active part in things. This became more difficult after new laws were passed in 1939.

Young Germans served in the Hitler Youth between the ages of 10 and 18. There were separate organisations for girls and boys.

The organisation of the Hitler Youth movement

AGE	BOYS	GIRLS
10 11 12 13	DEUTSCHES JUNGVOLK (DJ) German Young People ↓	JUNGMÄDELBUND (JM) League of Young Girls ↓
14 15 16 17 18	HITLER-JUGEND (HJ) Hitler Youth ↓	BUND DEUTSCHER MÄDEL (BDM) League of German Girls ↓

The main aim of the Hitler Youth was indoctrination. But it had other aims as well. It was used to prepare boys for service in the army. The girls' youth organisations were seen by the Nazis as less important than those for boys because girls did not do military

Hitler Youth trumpeter, 1935

service. The Hitler Youth was also a part of the machinery through which the Nazis kept watch on society. Its members were encouraged to report their teachers and even their parents for disloyalty.

SOURCE 91 — Hitler Youth on the march

SOURCE 92 — J. R. Tunis, American writer, 1936
The youth movement of the German Reich is called the Hitler-Jugend. This movement, started in 1926, is today part of the government with a huge organisation directed by a 29-year old leader, Baldur von Schirach . . . Boasting six million members, it is organised along military lines with squads, companies, battalions and regiments. Through 'Wehrsport', or military athletics, it aims to prepare the youth of Germany to step into the army trained and ready to fight. 'Wehrsport' includes marching, trench digging, use of dugouts, creeping under barbed wire, bayonet drill, gas defence and so forth . . .
(J. R. Tunis, "The Dictators Discover Sport", 'Foreign Affairs', July 1936)

▶ Of Sources 92, 93 and 94, which would you say is
 i.   most sympathetic
 ii. least sympathetic
towards Nazism?

SOURCE 93 — C. W. Domville-Fife, British writer, 1939
Life in the camp appeared to be one of healthy exercise at sports and games, but absolute discipline was maintained. By this I do not mean it was harshly enforced. It was, in fact, freely given by the boys themselves.

It seemed to me, also, that although every boy was conscious of his approaching military service, there was little if any regimentation or drill performed in the camp. The leader had, of course, served in the Army of the Reich: but as this is general with every man — and no German boy would respect anyone who had failed to do so — it can only be supposed that the Jugend has a certain thin strand of military enthusiasm interwoven in its bright, healthy and cheerful pattern of the German Boy Scout movement.
(C. W. Domville-Fife, 'This is Germany', Seeley, Service and Co, 1939)

Baldur von Schirach, Reich Youth Leader, 1933-40

▶ To what extent do Sources 95 and 96 support the claim made in Source 93 that life in the Hitler Youth movement was 'bright . . . and cheerful'?

SOURCE 94 — J. A. Cole, British writer, 1938

It is claimed that the work of the Hitler Youth is in no way a pre-military training. Whether this is theoretically true I cannot judge. . . All the same, I should think it is good preparation for the army. The children learn discipline. They march in ranks. They drill. I believe that, like boy scouts, they learn such accomplishments as signalling. When I attended a Hitler-Jugend meeting, I asked a boy what they had done on their last meeting-night. In the presence of several others and a superior he said pistol shooting. Very good fun and not necessarily a military pastime, but it hardly justifies the complete denial of all military associations. The aim of the Hitler-Jugend is stated to be education towards a National-Socialistic, healthy and efficient youth. That seems to me to be a fair statement of the aims and — to judge by externals — it is achieved.

(J. A. Cole, 'Just Back From Germany', Faber, 1938)

SOURCE 95 — Hitler Youth member, private letter, 1936

How did we live in Camp S —, which is supposed to be an example to all the other camps? We practically didn't have a minute of the day to ourselves. This isn't camp life, no sir! It's military barrack life! Drill starts right after a meagre breakfast with marmalade. We would like to have athletics, but there isn't any. Instead we have military exercises, down in the mud, till the tongue hangs out of your mouth; throwing of hand grenades, later 'theoretical' instruction about military tactics. The few hours which there isn't any military service are filled up by lectures. They call them 'political and cultural teachings'! They tell you things you've heard hundreds of times, about the 'genius and greatness of the Führer', about the 'soldier spirit of National Socialism'. And we have only one wish: sleep, sleep . . .

(S. Heym, "Youth in Hitler's Reich", 'The Nation', 27 June 1936)

SOURCE 96 — 'Germany Today', magazine published in Britain, 1938

The discipline of the HY in the district of western Germany is very much shaken. Many no longer want to be commandeered, but wish to do what they like. Usually only a third of the whole group appears for roll-call, although members get a list sent to their homes on which they have to signify that they have received notice of the meeting in good time. They are even threatened with expulsion from the HY for staying away, and this means very likely not getting jobs, or losing them. But the expulsions cannot be carried out because of the large number of members who do not attend. At evening meetings, it is a great event if 20 turn up out of 80, but usually there are only about 10 or 12. The level of these meetings is very low. They sing soldiers' songs and make a lot of noise, without doing any constructive work.

('Germany Today: News from Illegal Anti-Fascist Sources', May 1938)

Questions

1. Explain in your own words the aims of the Hitler Youth movement.
2. Which of the written sources in this Unit appears to be based on first-hand knowledge of the activities of the Hitler Youth, and which do not?
3. What do we learn from Sources 92-96 about the kind of activities that took place at Hitler Youth meetings and camps?
4. The Nazis denied that it was the purpose of the Hitler Youth to prepare boys for war. Which of the sources here support this claim, and which do not?
5. Study Source 96. State whether it contains
   i. only facts
   ii. only opinions
   iii. facts *and* opinions.
   Give reasons for your choice.

Education

Key ideas
1. The Nazis used schools for the purpose of indoctrination.
2. History and Biology were the school subjects most affected by the arrival in power of the Nazis.
3. Under the Nazis, schools placed special emphasis on Physical Education.

Core skills
1. Knowledge and understanding of educational arrangements under the Nazis.
2. Analysis of the motives which lay behind changes made to the school curriculum by the Nazis.

Schools in Nazi Germany were, like the Hitler Youth, used for the purpose of indoctrination. What this meant in practice was the teaching of a curriculum very different from the one which had been taught before Hitler came to power. History and Biology were among the subjects most affected. The Nazis insisted on more time being given to the study of History and Biology. They also laid down what was to be taught.

▶ In what ways would the account of German history 1914-33 set out in Source 97 have been disputed by a German Social Democrat?

SOURCE 97 — A British writer on Nazi history teaching, 1934

In 1933 a special course was decreed to explain the events of the National Revolution. The starting-point is the war, which is presented as a series of unbroken German victories. The breakdown is explained as 'the undermining of the German front by alien Marxist spies'. Then comes the revolution of 1918, organised by criminals and murderers; the Treaty of Versailles, bred from the hate of Germany's mortal enemies; the Dawes and Young Plans, the enslavement of Germany. Great emphasis is to be placed on the financial scandals of the Republic in which Jews were involved. Then comes the national resurgence with Hitler as the noble hero.
(R. Pascal, 'The Nazi Dictatorship, George Routledge, 1934)

SOURCE 98 — An order from the Nazi education minister, 1935

Racial instruction is to begin with the youngest pupils (six years of age) in accordance with the desire of the Führer that 'no boy or girl should leave school without complete knowledge of the necessity and meaning of blood purity' . . . Scholars must be acquainted with the most important results of research in the problems of heredity. Older scholars must have the importance of a choice of mate suitably explained to them, as being the only means of exercising influence on the hereditary and racial quality of posterity. The dangers of race-mingling with alien groups, especially non-European groups, must be portrayed with emphasis, because all inter-mixture with alien races . . . means ultimate decline.
(quoted in 'The Times', 29 January 1935)

The process of indoctrination did not, of course, end with History and Biology. The teaching of all subjects, even Maths and Science, was influenced by the Nazis' determination to shape the minds of the younger generation.

Der Stürmer, the most viciously
anti-Semitic of the Nazi newspapers, in use
in the classroom.

SOURCE 99 — A Nazi arithmetic problem

A squadron of 45 bombers drops incendiary bombs, each bomb
weighing 1.5 kilos. What is the total weight of the bomb load and
how many fires will be caused if one-third of the bombs hit their
objective and 20% of these hits result in fires?
('Germany Today', April 1939)

SOURCE 100 — An American writer on Nazi science textbooks, 1941

Dr E. Gunther's 'Physics of War' includes the following topics: (1)
observation, measurement and aiming; (2) instruction on shots; (3)
military aviation science; (4) engineer mechanics; bridge building;
(5) weather science; (6) various gas masks. 'Chemistry
Experiments for Schools' (1939) by Dr W. Kintoff contains the
following: 'Chapter I, Incendiary and Smoke Material; (1)
incendiary; phosphorus; (2) thermite; electro-thermite; (3)
chemical fire extinguishers. Chapter II, Breathing and Gas Masks;
(1) general infecting gas; (2) lung poison and choking gas; (3) skin
poison; (4) nose and throat gas.'
(I. L. Kandel, 'Educational Yearbook of the International Institute of Teachers'
College', Columbia University, 1941)

▶ What do you suppose the Nazis were
trying to achieve by teaching Maths and
Science in this way?

SOURCE 101 — Geography lesson as seen by a Nazi cartoonist

▶ What topic is being dealt with on the
blackboard?

▶ Suggest what other topics might have
appeared in the Nazi geography
syllabus.

The subject which changed most in status under the Nazis was Physical Education. It was given an importance that it had never previously enjoyed. The amount of time spent on PE in schools was trebled during the 1930s. This was in line with views expressed by Hitler in 'Mein Kampf'.

SOURCE 102 — Hitler on the need for physical education, 1925
A man of little scientific education but physically healthy, with a good, firm character, imbued with determination and willpower is more valuable to the national community than a clever weakling. A people of scholars, if they are physically degenerate, weak-willed and cowardly pacifists, will not storm the heavens . . . Not a day should go by in which the young man does not receive one hour's physical training . . . Sport does not exist only to make the individual strong, agile and bold; it should also toughen him and teach him to bear hardships.
(ed. D. C. Watt, 'Hitler's Mein Kampf', Hutchinson, 1969)

▶ What were the Nazis' motives for giving more time to PE?

▶ How did these motives differ in the case of boys and girls?

▶ How do they compare with the reasons you have to do PE?

SOURCE 103 — A Nazi official on PE for girls
The pre-requisite for future mothers of the nation must be sound physical training during girlhood . . . This can be effected by biological instruction, gymnastics, athletics and walking tours.
(H. P. Bleuel, 'Strength Through Joy', Secker & Warburg, 1973)

One task the Nazis did not entrust to the ordinary schools was the training of future leaders. They set up special schools for this purpose. Over thirty National Political Educational Institutions ('Napolas') were created to educate the next generation of administrators and army chiefs. After 1936 the 'Napolas' were run by the SS. Potential political leaders were trained in a handful of 'Adolf Hitler Schools' controlled by the Hitler Youth. The best products of these schools went on to further training at four 'Order Castles'.

Questions
1. What beliefs and attitudes did the Nazis try to instil among German young people concerning
   i. Adolf Hitler
   ii. Jews
   iii. warfare?
2. What attitude do you think the Nazis took towards the teaching in schools of
   i. religious knowledge
   ii. foreign languages like English and French?
3. In the late 1930s industrialists and others began to complain about the low standards of achievement in German schools. How would you account for these low standards?
4. In what ways do you think the Nazi education system would have been criticised by a political opponent of the Nazi régime?

Women in Nazi Germany

Key ideas
1. The Nazis had very firm ideas about the proper role of women in society.
2. In Nazi Germany women came under pressure to have children and to give up paid work.

Core skills
1. Knowledge and understanding of the role of women in Nazi society.
2. Interpretation and evaluation of a range of primary sources relating to the role of women in Nazi Germany.

The Nazi party was dominated by men. Its leaders nevertheless said that they believed in equality between men and women. They did not, however, suggest that men and women should do the same sort of jobs and lead the same sort of lives. They argued that men and women had different roles. These roles, however, were said to be of equal importance.

▶ What can you learn from these sources about Nazi views of the role of women?

▶ What evidence is there in Sources 105 and 106 which suggests that the Nazis did not really believe that men and women were 'on an equality'?

SOURCE 104 — Adolf Hitler, speaking in 1935
In the Germanic nations there has never been anything else than equality of rights for women. Both sexes had their rights, their tasks, and these tasks were in the case of each equal in dignity and value, and therefore man and woman were on an equality.
(N. Baynes, 'Speeches of Adolf Hitler', vol I, Oxford University Press, 1942)

SOURCE 105 — Goebbels, writing in 1929
The mission of women is to be beautiful and to bring children into the world. This is not at all as . . . unmodern as it sounds. The female bird pretties herself for her mate and hatches eggs for him. In exchange, the male takes care of gathering the food, and stands guard and wards off the enemy.
(ed. R. Bridenthal et al, "When Biology Became Destiny", 'Monthly Review', 1984)

SOURCE 106 — Rudolf Hess, leading Nazi, speaking in 1936
What National Socialists want are women who are genuine comrades and mothers. We do not want a limited, even characterless being, but a woman who is competent to stand by her man's side in complete understanding of his interests and life-struggle — a woman who can make his life more beautiful and richer in content. The ideal woman is one who, above all, is capable of being a mother . . . We are opposed to women going into professions which make them repulsive or 'mannified' or ridiculous caricatures.
(quoted in 'The Times', 27 May 1936)

A lot of pressure was put on women in the 1930s to have children and to give up work. One reason for this was Hitler's belief that Germany had to increase its population if it was to become more powerful. Women were given generous social security benefits and interest-free loans if they had children and left work. They were even given medals.

SOURCE 107 — The Mother Cross

Gold crosses were awarded to women who had more than eight children; silver to those who had more than six; and bronze to those who had more than four. Wearers of the 'Mother Cross' were entitled to a special salute from Hitler Youth and to an honoured place at Nazi meetings.

▶ Do these sources help us to understand whether German mothers were really honoured citizens in the way Source 107 suggests?

SOURCE 108 — Toni Christen, American journalist, 1939

I had seen Mrs Schmidt occasionally in the stores where I did my shopping. The day I talked to her she came out of a drugstore, a woman of about 50 years old. 'You see, older women are no good in Germany', she said. 'We are no longer capable of bearing children. We have no value to the state . . . They don't care for us mothers or grandmothers any more. We are worn out, discarded.'
(Toni Christen, "Women Without Hope", 'The Nation', 2 December 1939)

SOURCE 109 — Dr Leonore Kuhn, German writer, 1934

A young son, even the youngest, already laughs at his mother with 'manly' superiority if she, rather than his father, attempts to exercise authority over him. Instinctively he recognises his advantage from observing the subservience to which his mother has been reduced.
(quoted in 'The Nation', 12 September 1934)

There was another reason why the Nazis wanted women to leave work and have children. They aimed to bring down the unemployment figures by getting women to give up their jobs and replacing them with out-of-work men.

SOURCE 110 — Judith Grunfeld, American journalist, 1937

Hitler had no difficulty in passing laws making women class B subjects. The law of June 1933 states frankly the intention to relieve unemployment by eliminating women workers. What are the results of this crusade? How many women workers did the Führer send home? According to the statistics of the German Department of Labour, there were in June 1936 5,470,000 employed women, or 1,200,000 more than in January 1933 when Hitler came to power. The vigorous campaign against the employment of women has not led to their increased domesticity and security, but has been effective in squeezing them out of better-paid positions into the sweated trades. Needless to say, this type of labour, with its miserable wages and long hours is extremely dangerous to the health of women and degrades the family.
(Judith Grunfeld, "Women Workers in Nazi Germany", 'The Nation', 13 March 1937)

▶ Did German women in the 1930s give up paid work and become housewives in the way that the Nazis planned?

SOURCE 111 — 'Women, this is what your life is like in the Third Reich': Social Democrat Party poster

▶ Does this source give a more accurate impression of the status of women in Nazi Germany than Source 106?

Questions

1. Can you suggest reasons why an historian might regard Source 108 as a more useful and reliable piece of evidence than Source 109?
2. Does Source 110 contain
   i. only facts?
   ii. only opinions?
   iii. facts *and* opinions?
   Give reasons for your answer.
3. If you were writing a piece of anti-Nazi propaganda about the treatment of women in Germany during the 1930s, which *one* of the sources in this Unit would you find most useful? Explain what use you would make of the source you choose in your piece of propaganda.
4. 'Under the Nazis women were second-class citizens'. Explain the reasons why this was so.

Work and Leisure

Key ideas
1. The Nazis set up the German Labour Front to replace the outlawed trades union.
2. The 'Strength through Joy' movement was set up by the Nazis to organise workers' leisure time.

Core skills
1. Knowledge and understanding of the role of the Labour Front in Nazi Germany.
2. Interpretation of a range of primary sources relating to the activities of the Labour Front in Nazi Germany.

The German working class had in general opposed Nazism before 1933. The Nazis therefore paid special attention to the working classes when they came into power. They outlawed trade unions in 1933 as part of the process of 'co-ordination'. The trade unions were replaced by the 'Deutsche Arbeitsfront' (DAF) — the German Labour Front. The head of the DAF was Dr Robert Ley.

▶ Refer back to Source 16. To what extent does Source 16 support the claims made in Source 112 concerning the attachment of German workers to socialism and communism?

SOURCE 112 — The American Consul, Berlin, December 1933

The old labor unions with Socialist and Communist tendencies were incompatible with the new order of things, and as far as organisation is concerned they were wiped out. However, it was realised by the authorities that among the great mass of workers in Germany almost ineradicable political opinions of a Socialist and Communist nature were held by millions of individuals . . . Not only was it necessary to annihilate officially such organisations, but to commence a vigorous campaign to bring members into line with National Socialist principles. . .

(Foreign Relations of the United States, vol II, 1933)

SOURCE 113 — Germany Today, magazine published in Britain, July 1938

The German Labour Front (DAF) is not a trades union in the democratic sense of the word. In National Socialist Germany every employee must be a member of the German Labour Front, otherwise he would lose his job. The Labour Front is, however, not only a compulsory organisation, it is constituted on the National Socialist principle of 'leadership'. Not only are the employees members, but also the employers, and to the latter all power and rights over the employees are given by law. The employer is the 'leader of industry' and the staff at his works are his body of followers.

For every industrial district the National Socialist Government has appointed a so-called 'labour trustee' who is naturally a strict Nazi. This person, together with the employers, fixes the wage scale in his industrial district in all branches of industry.

The German Labour Front is intended to wipe out all social and class antagonism between employer and worker. It is to create 'social peace' as the Nazis call it. The Labour Front is to prevent all strikes, all struggles for better wages. A strike is 'the breaking of industrial peace' and as such is punishable by law . . .Further, the Labour Front aims to influence the masses in favour of National Socialism (by lectures, courses of study etc.) and to create among them a war mentality.

Robert Ley

Another organisation which, like the DAF, was intended to play a part in breaking down class barriers was the Reichsarbeitsdienst (RAD) — the National Labour Service. In 1935 Hitler made it compulsory for 18-25 year old German men to do six months' service in the RAD. He said that people from different backgrounds would be bound together by their RAD service. This did not happen. The RAD was unpopular with those who had to serve in it. The work — usually on building projects — was exhausting. The pay was meagre and living conditions were very poor.

The Nazis were not content with controlling people's lives at work. They also set out to organise people's free time. The organisation that was created to do this was called Kraft durch Freude (KdF) — 'Strength through Joy'. The KdF was part of Ley's Labour Front.

RAD stamp, 1944

SOURCE 114 — Nazi report on the activities of the KdF in the Berlin area, 1933-38

SPONSORED EVENTS		PARTICIPANTS
21,146	Theatre performances	11,507,432
989	Concerts	705,623
20,527	Cultural events of various forms	10,518,282
93	Exhibitions	2,435,975
61,503	Tours through museums and factories	2,567,596
19,060	Courses and lectures of the German Adult Education Office	1,009,922
388	Sports events	1,432,596
1,196	Holiday trips and cruises	702,491
3,499	Week-end trips	1,007,242
5,896	Hikes	126,292

▶ What can you learn from Sources 114-116 about
  i. the range of KdF activities?
  ii. the popularity of the KdF activities?

SOURCE 115 — C. W. Domville-Fife, British writer, 1939
Under the auspices of 'Strength through Joy' the German worker can attend theatres, concerts and educational courses, at prices well within his means; he can take part in sports previously the preserve of the well-to-do; and, possibly the most widely known of all features of this movement, he can travel through his own country or abroad at incredibly low cost . . . This 'Joy' movement . . . has achieved enormous popularity and strength.
(C. W. Domville-Fife, 'This is Germany', Seeley, Service & Co, 1939)

SOURCE 116 — Social Democratic Party report on public opinion in Berlin, 1938
Strength through Joy is very popular. The events appeal to the yearning of the little man who wants an opportunity to get out and about and to take part in the pleasures of the 'top people' . . . For such a man it really means something to have been on a trip to Scandinavia . . . he imagines that he has thereby climbed up a rung on the social ladder.
(J. Noakes and G. Pridham, 'Nazi Germany 1919-45, vol 3', Exeter University Press, 1984)

The KdF did not confine itself to trips and concerts. It also got involved in a scheme to enable German workers to buy their own car. This was the Volkswagen ('people's car') project. Ley persuaded large numbers of people to start paying for cars on hire purchase before the Volkswagen factory went into production. None of these customers had received a car by the time war broke out in 1939. The Volkswagen plant was then turned over to weapons production. None of the money paid in by would-be buyers was ever refunded.

Hitler inspects a model of the 'people's car'.

Questions
1. What can you learn from Source 113 about relations between the Nazis and Germany's businessmen and employers?
2. How did the way that wages were fixed in Nazi Germany differ from the way in which they are fixed in countries which have free trade unions?
3. How free were workers in Nazi Germany to take industrial action in an attempt to improve their wages?

4. Would you agree that the author of Source 115 was a supporter of the Nazis? Explain your answer by referring to language and tone as well as to the content of the source.
5. 'For Germany's workers the benefits of Nazi rule outweighed the disadvantages.' To what extent do the sources in this Unit offer support for this view?

The Nazi Economy

Key ideas
1. Hitler wanted to bring down unemployment in Germany and, on paper, succeeded.
2. After 1933 the Nazis created a 'war economy' in Germany.
3. Hitler wanted Germany to be economically self-sufficient.

Core skills
1. Knowledge and understanding of Nazi economic policies.
2. Analysis of the consequences of Nazi policy for the German economy and for the German people.

Hitler was not greatly interested in economics. When in power he did not get closely involved in the business of running Germany's economy. Instead he made it clear what he wanted and then left it to others to work out in detail how his demands were to be met. In the 1930s Hitler set those responsible for the economy three tasks. One was to reduce unemployment. Another was to organise things so as to allow Germany's armed forces to be enlarged and re-equipped. The third was to make Germany economically self-sufficient.

Unemployment and Living Stardards

Hitler's determination to reduce unemployment did not have so much to do with concern for the welfare of those who were jobless as it did with concern about his own personal prestige. In the late 1920s and early 1930s the Nazis had been scornful about the failure of German governments to cope with rising unemployment. In the 1933 election campaign Hitler had promised to beat unemployment within four years. Failure to keep his promise would have left him looking foolish. In addition Nazi Germany as a whole would have looked foolish if it had failed to tackle the problem of unemployment more effectively than the governments of the Weimar Republic.

The Nazi government created jobs by spending money. Private firms were given financial help by the government in order to get a house-building programme under way. The government itself launched a big road-building programme. The motorways (autobahnen) that were built became known as 'Adolf Hitler's highways'.

SOURCE 117 — Hitler, speaking in September 1933
6400 kilometres of new motor roads are being planned as the first step in the fight against unemployment. This fight must be waged because we have promised the nation that we will remove its present distress . . . The best possible way to bring the German people back to work is, as I see it, to set German economic life once more in motion through great monumental works.

(N. Baynes, 'Speeches of Adolf Hitler, vol I', Oxford University Press, 1942)

▶ Did Hitler have any reason other than reducing unemployment for building motorways?

The unemployment figures came down sharply during Hitler's first years in power. The Nazis were quick to boast of their success in what they called the 'battle of labour'. There are, however, reasons for doubting just how genuine this success was.

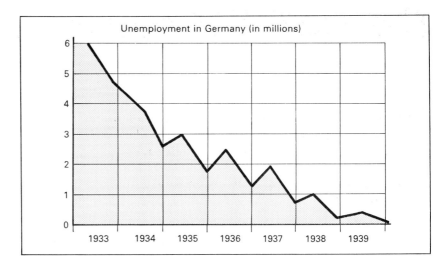

Unemployment in Germany (in millions)

Unemployment in Germany, 1933-39

SOURCE 118 — Norman Thomas, American writer, 1936

Under the Nazis there has been much 'invisible unemployment'. The number of unemployed Jews is great and is increasing: but these are not counted as unemployed. Another source of 'invisible unemployment' has been the wholesale discharge of women . . . and of unmarried men under the age of 25. None of these are included among the unemployed in the official statistics. Part-time workers are counted as fully employed. The reintroduction of conscription has taken hundreds of thousands of young men off the labour market.

(Norman Thomas, "Labour under the Nazis", 'Foreign Affairs', April 1936)

SOURCE 119 — 'Germany Today', magazine published in Britain, 1938

According to official statistics there are in Germany about one million unemployed as compared with somewhat over two million at the end of 1928. No other big industrial country can boast today of the fact that its number of unemployed is lower than before the crisis. How has Hitler performed this miracle? Quite simply. Instead of paying the unemployed a dole he has put them into the army or other kinds of forced service, such as labour service, land service and so on. The army today is larger than before by about 750,000 men . . .

▶ A leading historian has called the Nazi victory in the 'battle of labour' a 'sham success'. How far would you agree with this view?

The reduction of unemployment in Nazi Germany — however genuine — was certainly not accompanied by a big improvement in standards of living. Foreign critics of Nazism often claimed that ordinary Germans were not as well off under Hitler as they were in the years of the Weimar Republic. It was said, quite rightly, that under the Nazis prices went up and hours of work were longer. There were, however, wage rises as well as price rises.

SOURCE 120 — Consumption per head of selected foods, 1929-37

	1929	1932	1937
Meat (kg)	44.9	42.1	45.9
Butter (kg)	8.0	7.5	8.9
Eggs (units)	141	138	122
Potatoes (kg)	172	191	174
Tropical fruits (kg)	7.8	8.0	5.8
Beer (litres)	88.6	51.4	62.9

▶ What people spend their money on — what they consume — gives a good idea of what is happening to their standard of living. Do these figures suggest that living standards rose or fell in Nazi Germany?

SOURCE 121 — 'What? Bread? Don't you know the National Socialist revolution is over?' (Cartoon from Humanité, French newspaper, 1934)
'Freedom and bread' was a Nazi slogan in the 1920s.

▶ What message do you think the cartoonist is trying to put across?

Rearmament

In the 1920s Hitler had endlessly attacked the Versailles treaty and the restrictions it placed on Germany's armed forces. When he came into power in 1933 he was determined to rearm as quickly as possible. Rearmament not only meant bigger armed forces but also the large-scale production of weapons like tanks and bombers which were banned under the Versailles treaty. Under the Nazis the German economy was reshaped so that it became what was called a 'war economy' ('Wehrwirtschaft').

SOURCE 122 — Record of a German cabinet meeting, 8 February 1933

The Reich Chancellor [Hitler] stated that . . . the next five years in Germany had to be devoted to rendering the German people again capable of bearing arms . . .

The War Minister [von Blomberg] expressed the point of view that . . . the immediate needs of the Army had to be considered. The German Army was disarmed to such an extent that the prime necessity was to provide the material foundation for armaments. Only after emergency armaments had been completed would it be possible to tackle larger tasks . . .

The Reich Chancellor again stressed that for the next 4-5 years the main principle had to be: everything for the armed forces. Germany's position in the world depended decisively on the position of the German armed forces.
(J. Noakes and G. Pridham, 'Nazism 1919-45, vol 2', Exeter University Press, 1984)

In the early 1930s the Nazis wanted to keep the extent of German rearmament secret so as not to upset Britain and France. They also had the problem of paying for rearmament at a time when the government's income from taxes was low because of the depression. These problems were solved by Dr Hjalmar Schacht.

Hjalmar Schacht

Schacht was chief of Germany's national bank (1933-39) and Hitler's Minister of Economics (1934-7). Schacht paid arms manufacturers with things called 'mefo bills'. These were secret government credit notes that manufacturers could cash at the national bank. This method of paying for weaponry fell into disuse after Hitler decided in 1935 that German rearmament no longer needed to be kept secret.

Schacht, wizard in finance though he was, did not last very long as Hitler's economic dictator. He began to complain in the mid-1930s that the Nazis were going too fast in their efforts to build a 'war economy'. Hitler pushed him aside. His place as economic dictator was taken by Goering.

In the 1930s Hermann Goering was generally reckoned to be the second most important person in the Nazi party after Hitler himself. He had a number of posts. He was, among other things, president of the Reichstag, head of the state of Prussia and chief of the new German air force or Luftwaffe. In 1936 Hitler put him in charge of the new Four Year Plan as well. The aim of the Four Year Plan was to drive Germany's economy in the direction of autarky.

Goering had no real qualifications for the task of running the German economy. He had no background in economics or business. He was a first world war fighter pilot who had become a full-time politician in the 1920s.

Hermann Goering

Autarky

'Autarky' means economic self-sufficiency. A country which is economically self-sufficient is one which can meet all its own needs without having to rely on imports from other countries. Hitler wanted Germany to be economically self-sufficient so that it could win wars. He remembered the way in which Germany had been worn down during the first world war by the effects of the Allied blockade. Ships carrying food and raw materials had been unable to get into German ports.

▶ Did the Nazis have a reason other than the one given in the text for aiming at autarky?

SOURCE 123 — Hitler speaking in 1936

In four years Germany must be completely independent of foreign countries so far as concerns those materials which by any means through German skill, through our chemical industry or through our mining industry we can ourselves produce. Further, the development of this great German raw material industry will, within the national economy, usefully employ supplies of labour which will be set free on the completion of rearmament.

(N. Baynes, 'Speeches of Adolf Hitler, vol I', Oxford University Press, 1942)

The drive towards autarky involved the production of 'ersatz' materials. 'Ersatz' materials are artificial substitutes for things that occur naturally. Under the Four Year Plan the Nazis made a big effort to produce large quantities of 'ersatz' rubber and oil. They did not meet the ambitious targets they set themselves but they did have quite a lot of success.

Hitler realised that Germany could not become completely self-sufficient on the basis of 'ersatz' materials alone. He recognised that in order to become fully self-sufficient Germany had to win control of new supplies of things like oil and wheat. The only way this could be done was by conquering other countries. The idea of trying to produce 'ersatz' materials was to tide Germany over until these conquests could take place.

Questions

1. Write a sentence to explain the meaning of each of the following: autobahnen; Wehrwirtschaft; mefo bills; autarky; ersatz materials.
2. Put the following events into the correct chronological sequence:
   a. the beginning of the Four Year Plan,
   b. the start of the road-building programme,
   c. Schacht's appointment as Minister for Economics,
   d. the announcement of German rearmament,
   e. unemployment in Germany fell to under one million.
3. Which do you think Hitler saw as the most urgent task — reducing unemployment, rearming or making Germany economically self-sufficient? Give reasons for your answer.
4. 'It was a mistake on Hitler's part to dismiss Schacht as economic supremo, and another mistake to give the job to Goering'. What arguments can be offered in support of this view?
5. 'The Nazis were more concerned with increasing Germany's prestige than they were with bringing about prosperity'. Does the evidence contained in this Unit suggest that this statement is correct? Give reasons for your answer.

The Nazis and the Jews

Key ideas

1. In 1935 German Jews were deprived of German citizenship.
2. In 1938 Germany's Jews were the victims of a pogrom.
3. During the war the Nazis set out to kill all of the Jews in occupied Europe.

Core skills

1. Knowledge and understanding of the main stages in the Nazi war against the Jews.
2. Empathetic understanding of the responses of German Jews and non-Nazi Germans to Nazi anti-semitism.
3. Interpretation of a range of primary sources relating to Nazi anti-semitism during the 1930s.

In the 1920s and early 1930s foreigners working in Germany as diplomats or journalists sometimes suggested that if Hitler got into power he would become respectable and leave anti-semitism behind. This did not happen. When in power the Nazis put their anti-semitic beliefs savagely into practice. Winston Churchill, Britain's wartime Prime Minister, described their treatment of the Jews as the 'the most horrible single crime ever committed in the whole history of the world'.

In 1933 there were about half a million Jews living in Germany. It should not be thought that they were a group of people who somehow lived apart from the rest of the population. 100,000 German Jews had fought and died alongside non-Jews in the German army during the first world war. In the 1920s the Jewish community provided the Weimar Republic with some of its most celebrated citizens. Nazi claims that Jews controlled the political and economic life of the Weimar Republic were pure fantasy. Most members of Germany's Jewish community lived ordinary quiet lives. They were on average neither richer nor poorer than the rest of Germany's population.

Persecution

When the Nazis came into power in 1933 the SA went on the rampage against Germany's Jews. Jews were attacked and beaten on the streets. These attacks were not ordered by Hitler but were the work of local SA commanders acting on their own initiative. The first official attack made on Germany's Jews came in the form of a boycott of Jewish shops ordered by Hitler for 1 April 1933.

▶ Pick out from the following words the three which best describe the frame of mind of the author of this source — terrified, surprised, stunned, bewildered, bitter, calm, apprehensive, contemptuous, angry, forgiving.

SOURCE 124 — Private letter by 'J', a Jewish refugee, 1933

This is what Boycott Saturday looked like in Germany: All Jewish stores and offices were placarded with posters saying: 'Germans don't buy from Jews!'; 'No German visits a Jewish doctor'; 'He who buys in this Jewish store will be photographed' . . . Wherever you go and whomever you see of your friends, you find sorrowful people. Nearly everyone, no, everyone is faced with the question, What will happen to us, how shall we live? Dr K. has been discharged from the hospital; Dr W. has been fired from his school — the pupils refused to answer him in his classes. The lawyers were barred from the courts, the judges were all dismissed, all doctors were removed from the hospitals, nobody was allowed to buy from Jews. And if one is lucky enough to have escaped the German inferno, and to find oneself in Switzerland where everything is so calm and peaceful, then one has to ask oneself:

Anti-semitic beer mat of the 1930s. The writing says, 'Whoever buys from a Jew is a national traitor'.

How is it possible? Did I have a nightmare? I forgot to tell you that on that blackest of all Saturdays big trucks patrolled the Berlin streets from which Nazis shouted down through loudspeakers: 'Down with the Jews!'; 'Jews, die like beasts!' One of the most popular songs of these inhuman beasts was: 'If Jewish blood flows from the knife, things will go much better.' The words for this song were written by the Nazi poet Horst Wessel.
('The Nation', 26 April 1933)

There were other anti-Jewish moves in 1933 apart from the one-day shops boycott. The most important of these was a law which forced Jews out of the German civil service. The next year, 1934, saw something of a pause in Nazi persecution of the Jews. Hitler then returned to the attack. In 1935 the so-called Nuremberg Laws were passed. The purpose of these laws was to make Germany's Jews a separate and isolated group in society. There were two Nuremberg Laws. One was called the 'Reich Citizenship Law'. This deprived Jews of German citizenship and turned them into aliens or 'guests' in their own country. The other was called the 'Law for the Protection of German Blood and Honour'. This outlawed marriages between Jews and non-Jews. It also made sexual relations outside marriage between Jews and non-Jews a criminal offence punishable by imprisonment.

In the five years after Hitler came to power Jews in Germany were viciously persecuted. Over 200 were murdered. Large numbers emigrated. In the 1930s half of Germany's Jewish population left the country. Others stayed. Perhaps they thought that after the Nuremberg Laws things could not get worse. They were wrong.

The shops boycott

Pogrom

Clearing up after 'Crystal Night'.

► In what way was Germany's Jewish community attacked on 'Crystal Night'?

► Who exactly carried out the atrocities of 'Crystal Night'?

► What conclusions can be reached on the basis of these sources about the attitude of ordinary Germans to the events of 'Crystal Night'?

East German stamp issued on the 25th anniversary of 'Crystal Night'. It depicts a burning synagogue.

In November 1938 a Jewish student went into the German embassy in Paris and shot dead the first official he saw. He wanted to take revenge for the way in which his family had been treated in Germany. The Nazis used this killing as an excuse to launch a pogrom against Germany's Jews. A pogrom is an organised assault on an entire community. The Nazis called their pogrom 'Kristallnacht' ('Crystal Night') because so much glass was broken.

SOURCE 125 — New York Times, American newspaper, 11 November 1938

A wave of destruction . . . swept over Germany today. Huge crowds looked on . . . Generally the crowds were silent and the majority seemed gravely disturbed by the proceedings. Only members of the wrecking squads shouted occasionally 'Perish Jewry!' and 'Kill the Jews!' though in one case a person in the crowd shouted 'Why not hang the owner in the window?' In some cases on the other hand crowds were observed making passages for Jews to leave their stores unmolested.

SOURCE 126 — News Chronicle, British newspaper, 11 November 1938

POGROM RAGES THROUGH GERMANY
INCENDIARY MOBS WRECK SHOPS, SYNAGOGUES

The rioting began in the early hours of this morning when formations of the Hitler Youth and Storm Troops streamed out of the taverns where they had been celebrating the fifteenth anniversary of Hitler's march on Munich. Drunken and aflame they set about their work of destruction. Synagogues were fired . . . Squads of youths, baffled by the stout doors, set ladders against the windows, broke the panes and jumped in with petrol cans. Meanwhile, bawling, raucous gangs stumbled through the streets hurling bricks and stones through the windows of Jewish shops. The worst scenes of destruction were on the Kurfürstendamm, a fashionable shopping centre . . . Here, in the early hours of the morning, while the average Berliner was trudging to work, looters smashed with peculiar care the windows of jewellery shops and, sniggering, stuffed into their pockets the trinkets and necklaces that fell to the pavement. The average Germans looked on either apathetic or astonished. They sidled past scenes of destruction half-ashamed . . . Physical assaults on Jews were witnessed in Berlin today. Single Jews were chased through the streets by young Nazis, pummelled and knocked down.

SOURCE 127 — The American Consul, Leipzig, November 1938

The shattering of shop windows, looting of stores and dwellings of Jews . . . was hailed subsequently in the Nazi press as a 'spontaneous wave of righteous indignation throughout Germany' . . . So far as a very high percentage of the German populace is concerned, a state of popular indignation that would spontaneously lead to such excesses, can be considered as non-existent. On the contrary, in viewing the ruins . . . all of the local crowds observed were obviously benumbed over what had happened and aghast over the unprecedented fury of the Nazi acts . . .

(J. Noakes and G. Pridham, 'Nazism 1919-45, vol 2', Exeter University Press, 1984)

During 'Crystal Night' nearly 100 Jews were killed. 30,000 others were arrested and sent to concentration camps.

The 1938 pogrom was followed by a rash of new anti-semitic laws. A communal fine of one *billion* marks was imposed on Germany's Jews for the Paris embassy murder. Jews were banned from running businesses and employing workers. Jewish children were excluded from schools. Jews were banned from many public places.

Genocide

What remained was the last and most horrifying phase of the Nazi war against the Jews. In 1941 Hitler decided to embark on a policy of genocide. Genocide means the deliberate and systematic extermination of a whole nation or community. The Nazis called their policy of genocide the 'final solution' of the Jewish question. It is referred to nowadays as 'the Holocaust'.

Only a small proportion of those who died in the Holocaust were German Jews. Most of its victims came from countries occupied by the Nazis during the second world war. Something like half of the six million Jews who died in the holocaust were Polish. Before the war the biggest Jewish communities in Europe were in Poland and in Russia.

After 1941 Jews in the countries of Nazi-occupied Europe were rounded up and taken to extermination camps. Most of these were in Poland. The camps at which most Jews were put to death were at Auschwitz, Treblinka, Sobibor, Belzec, Chelmno, and Majdanek.

Not all the Holocaust's victims died in the gas chambers of the extermination camps. Many were butchered in their home countries by the 'Einsatzgruppen'. Others were worked to death in labour camps. Some died in gruesome medical 'experiments' carried out by SS doctors.

Some two million of Europe's eight million Jews survived.

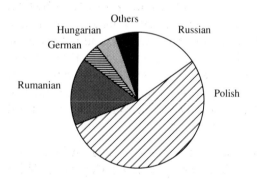

The nationalities of the victims of the Holocaust. The total number of victims was approximately six million.

Questions

1. Construct a time chart showing the main events in the Nazi war against the Jews.
2. Can you suggest reasons why many German Jews, despite persecution, were reluctant to leave Germany in the 1930s?
3. Source 126 is a factual report on the events of Crystal Night. The writer's attitude to these events can, however, be worked out from the language he uses to describe them. What was the writer's attitude to the events of Crystal Night, and how is it revealed in the language he uses?
4. An editorial is a short article in which a newspaper puts forward its opinions on political and other developments. Compose an editorial of the kind that might have appeared in the 'News Chronicle' on the day after Crystal Night.

Nazi Propaganda in the 1930s

Key ideas

1. After 1933 the media in Germany were controlled by the Nazis.
2. Under the Nazis Germans were subjected to a constant barrage of propaganda.
3. The Nuremberg rallies were the high point of the Nazi political calendar.

Core skills

1. Knowledge and understanding of Nazi propaganda in the 1930s.
2. Evaluation and interpretation of a range of primary source materials relating to Nazi propaganda in the 1930s.

When the Nazis came to power in 1933 Goebbels, the party's propaganda chief, was made Minister of Propaganda and National Enlightenment. Goebbels' task as Minister was rather different from the one he had had during what the Nazis called the 'Kampfzeit' (time of struggle). During the Kampfzeit his task had been to turn people into Nazi voters. His task after 1933 was to make sure that the Nazi regime retained popular support.

Goebbels had two main concerns as Minister of Propaganda. One was make sure that Germans did not see or read anything that was in any way hostile or damaging to Nazism. The other was to make sure that the Nazi view of things was put across in the most persuasive way possible.

Goebbels prevented the appearance of anything hostile to Nazism through an organisation he set up in 1933 called the Reich Chamber of Culture. The Chamber of Culture contained sections dealing with newspapers, film, radio, art, literature, theatre and music. People who wanted to work in these fields had to be members of the Chamber. Only those who were sympathetic to Nazism were admitted. People who were not admitted could not get their work published or performed.

The Nazis made it clear what they thought of non-Nazi and anti-Nazi writers in the book-burning episode of May 1933. With Goebbels in attendance, Berlin students ceremonially set fire to a huge pile of books which had been looted from libraries. In the pile were books by some of Germany's most famous authors.

Goebbels went to immense trouble to ensure that the Nazi message was put across in the most persuasive way possible. Journalists received detailed instructions about what news was to be printed in their papers. They were also given orders about what news was to be left out. Radio broadcasts were controlled in the same way. No film could go into production without Goebbels' approval.

Goebbels did not care very much whether things that were printed or broadcast were true or false. All that really mattered to him was whether what was put out served the Nazi cause.

SOURCE 128 — Goebbels, speaking in 1933

Propaganda is not an end in itself, but a means to an end. If the means achieves the end then the means is good. . . The new Ministry has no other aim than to unite the nation behind the ideal

Josef Goebbels

of the national revolution. If the aim has been achieved then people can pronounce judgement on my methods if they wish: that would be a matter of complete indifference, for the Ministry would then by its efforts have achieved its goal.

(J. Noakes and G. Pridham, 'Nazism 1919-45, vol 2', Exeter University Press, 1984)

SOURCE 129 — An example of Nazi propaganda — The Westfälische Landeszeitung, German newspaper, January 1939

▶ What does the upper map suggest about
  i. the position of Jews in the Weimar Republic?
  ii. the strength of the Communists during the years of the Weimar Republic? (note: the red star and the hammer and sickle are symbols of communism).
  iii. Germany's economic strength during the years of the Weimar Republic? (note: an 'Arbeitsamt' is a labour exchange or job centre).

▶ In the upper map, what do you think the Nazi on his knees holding the swastika flag is supposed to represent?

▶ What does the lower map suggest about
  i. the economic strength of Germany after 1933?
  ii. the military power of Germany after 1933?

Goebbels believed that the written word was not as effective as an instrument of propaganda as the spoken word or film. He therefore paid special attention to what was heard on the radio and what was seen in the cinemas.

The Nazis made sure that practically everyone had access to a radio. Radios could be bought very cheaply. They were installed in factories and offices so that people could hear important broadcasts during working hours. Loudspeakers were even put up in the streets.

Goebbels dealt with films in a devious way. He knew that German cinema audiences were unlikely to go and see crude or boring propaganda films. This was because they were used to films of a high standard. The 1920s had been a golden age in German film-making. Goebbels therefore allowed the film industry to produce lots of comedies and adventure films that contained

Hitlerjunge Quex poster, 1933

ɧitlerjunge Quex

The main celebrations in the Nazi political calendar

▶ How can you tell that this report is itself a piece of propaganda?

nothing to do with politics. He also made sure the political films that were produced were of high quality. One of the best known of these was "Hitlerjunge Quex", made in 1933. It told the story of a boy who broke away from a communist family and joined the Hitler Youth only to be murdered by the communists.

Another form of propaganda extensively used by the Nazis was the political celebration or ritual. Hitler and Goebbels had been aware of the value of rallies, marches and parades long before they came into power. They knew that at such events people could be spellbound or brainwashed. In Nazi Germany elaborately-staged celebrations or rituals were regular events.

Main celebrations in the Nazi political calendar	
January	Day of the Seizure of power
February	Founding of the Nazi Party Day
March	Heroes' Remembrance Day (remembrance of war dead)
April	Fuhrer's birthday
September	Party Rally, Nuremburg
November	Anniversary of the Munich Putsch

The annual party rally at Nuremberg was the great showpiece event of the Nazi year. It took place in a stadium designed by Hitler's architect, Albert Speer. The rally of 1937 was one of the most spectacular.

SOURCE 130 — Niederelbischen Tageblatt, German newspaper, 1937

The square of the Zepplinfeld was divided into about 20 columns in which about 140,000 political leaders were standing. Countless swastika flags were waving in the light evening breeze. A distant rumbling! The roaring comes closer and becomes louder! The Führer! And then a great surprise. As Adolf Hitler enters the Zepplinfeld, one hundred and fifty searchlights of the airforce are switched on. They have been stationed around the edge of the square, and they cut out and build a canopy of light from the darkness over the whole field . . . Is such a thing possible: a cathedral of light?　　(S. Taylor, 'Prelude to Genocide', Duckworth, 1985)

Political rituals probably had most effect on those Germans who were loyal Nazis. The effect of these rituals and of other forms of Nazi propaganda on ordinary Germans is not easy to judge.

SOURCE 131 — William Shirer, American journalist, writing in 1959

I myself was to experience how easily one is taken in by a lying and censored press and radio in a totalitarian state. Though unlike most Germans I had daily access to foreign newspapers . . . and though I listened regularly to the BBC and other foreign broadcasts, my job necessitated the spending of many hours a day in combing the German press, checking the German radio, conferring with Nazi officials and going to party meetings. It was surprising and sometimes consternating to find that notwithstanding the opportunities I had to learn the facts . . . a steady diet of falsification and distortions made a certain impression on one's mind and often misled it. No one who has not lived for years in a totalitarian land can possibly conceive how difficult it is to escape the consequences . . . of a regime's calculated and incessant propaganda.

(William L. Shirer, 'The Rise and Fall of the Third Reich', Secker & Warburg, 1960)

SOURCE 132 — The U.S. Ambassador in Germany, writing in 1936

A people so susceptible to the influence of mass suggestion is apt, under the spell of alluring promises held out by clever propagandists, to forget the less pleasant aspects of its existence. And here the resources of a marvellously organised Ministry of Propaganda has been of indisputable value. A systematic campaign of propaganda was inaugurated to break down the resistance of 'doubting Thomases' and to strengthen the enthusiasm of those already converted to the new order . . . With steam-roller effectiveness, the activities of the Ministry of Propaganda reached out into every corner of the Reich, into every walk of life.

('Foreign Relations of the United States, 1936, vol II')

SOURCE 133 — Social Democratic Party report on public opinion in North Germany, 1938

The most shocking thing is the ignorance of wide circles about what is actually going on in Germany . . . They are completely convinced that there are no longer concentration camps: they simply do not want to believe that the Nazis treat their opponents with ruthless brutality . . . The front against National Socialism could be much broader if people really knew what things are like in Germany. But this front is now very small even among the workers.

(J. Noakes and G. Pridham, 'Nazism 1919-45, vol 2', Exeter University Press)

SOURCE 134 — Social Democratic Party report on public opinion in Western Germany, 1936

A large section of the population no longer reads a newspaper. Basically, the population are indifferent to what is in the newspapers . . . The Nazis try, as they say, to turn everyone into committed National Socialists. They will never succeed in that. People tend rather to turn inwardly away from Nazism. But they are ensuring that people are no longer interested in anything.

(J. Noakes and G. Pridham, op. cit.)

SOURCE 135 — Social Democratic Party report on public opinion in Eastern Germany, 1938

One cannot speak of popular enthusiasm for Nazism. Only the school children and . . . those young men who have not yet done their military service are enthusiastic about Hitler.

(J. Noakes and G. Pridham, op. cit.)

Questions

1. Explain in your own words the role of
   i. the Reich Chamber of Culture
   ii. the Nuremberg rallies in Nazi Germany.
2. How would you describe the aims of the person who produced Source 129 (the Westfälische Landeszeitung map)?
3. Would you agree that Sources 131 and 132 take much the same view concerning the effectiveness of Nazi propaganda? Give reasons for your answer.
4. Would you agree that the impression of the effectiveness of Nazi propaganda given in Source 134 is different from that given in Sources 131 and 132? Give reasons for your answer.
5. Sources 133-35 were written by undercover Social Democrat agents working in Germany for their party's leaders who were living in exile. What do you think are
   i. the strengths
   ii. the weaknesses of this evidence from the point of view of the historian?
6. In Source 128 Goebbels says that his aim was 'to unite the nation behind . . . the national revolution'. Does the evidence contained in this Unit lead you to believe that he achieved this aim
   i. fully
   ii. partly or
   iii. not at all?

Resistance to Nazism

Key ideas
1. In the 1930s what resistance there was to Nazism came from Social Democrats and Communists.
2. In the 1940s there was upper class resistance to Nazism as well.

Core skills
1. Knowledge of German resistance to Nazi rule.
2. Analysis of the resistance to Nazi rule making use of the concepts of similarity and difference.

It is difficult to say how much opposition there was to Nazism in Germany after 1933. There are no public opinion poll results to tell us. It is probable that the number of people who disliked Nazism was very large. There is, however, a difference between disliking something and actively opposing it. The number of people who either protested openly against Nazism or who tried to overthrow it was very small. These people — those who resisted Nazism — were people of extraordinary bravery. The penalty for resistance was at the very least detention in a concentration camp and was normally death. Most people who disliked but did not resist Nazism appear to have tried to shut themselves off from what was happening. This became known as 'inner emigration'.

The 1930s

In the 1930s what resistance to Nazism there was came from within the churches and from the remains of the two left-wing political parties, the Communists and the Social Democrats.

The Communists and Social Democrats were, of course, outlawed in 1933. The leaders of the two parties either went into exile or were put into concentration camps. Both parties, though, were able to set up an 'underground' organisation inside Germany. The two underground organisations did not co-operate with each other. This may seem surprising. The two organisations were, after all, trying to spread the idea of resistance among the same sort of people — the factory workers. The problem was that the Communists and Social Democrats did not trust each other. The main reason for this was that the Communist resisters had close links with the Soviet Union. They saw the collection of information that was helpful to the Soviet Union as an important part of their job. This work was done through spy rings like the Rote Kapelle (the 'Red Orchestra'). The Social Democrat resisters had no interest in spying for the Soviet Union. They were enemies of Moscow-style communism.

Neither the Communist nor the Social Democratic underground was able to offer anything very much in the way of effective resistance.

SOURCE 136 — Gestapo report, 1937
During the first years after the take-over of power the Communists tried to expand their party . . . But later they saw clearly that they only endangered those members illegally active inside the country . . . Whereas until 1936 the main propaganda emphasis was on

▶ What were the similarities and differences between Communist and Social Democrat resistance in the 1930s?

distributing lots of pamphlets, at the beginning of 1936 they switched to propaganda by word of mouth . . . The illegal activity of the SPD is the same as that . . . of the Communists . . . Since the former SPD members carry on propaganda only by word of mouth, it is very difficult to get hold of proof of their illegal activities.
(J. Noakes and G. Pridham, 'Nazism 1919-45, vol 2', Exeter University Press, 1984)

The 1940s

In the 1940s, as in the 1930s, members of the Catholic and Protestant churches were prominent in the resistance to Nazism. Count Galen, the Catholic bishop of Münster, spoke out against the Nazis in his sermons. Dietrich Bonhoeffer, a Protestant clergyman, involved himself in plans to overthrow Hitler. He was arrested in 1943 and executed in 1945.

There were also young people who called for the overthrow of Hitler. In Munich a group of university students calling themselves the 'White Rose' wrote and handed out leaflets condemning the evils of Nazism. The leaders of the 'White Rose' were Hans and Sophie Scholl. They and their friends were arrested and executed in 1943.

Some of the bravest and most determined resistance in the 1940s came from members of Germany's upper class. There were two upper-class resistance organisations: the 'Kreisau Circle' and the 'Beck-Goerdeler group'.

These upper-class resisters had for the most part been quite friendly towards Nazism in the 1930s. This was mainly because they were nationalists. They hoped the Nazis could make Germany great and powerful again. Why did they change their minds about the Nazis? There were several reasons. One was the brutality of Nazi rule. Another was the greed of the Nazi leaders. Probably most important was the fear that Hitler's war policies would lead to Germany being ruined.

The 'Kreisau Circle' took its name from the country home of its leader, Helmuth von Moltke. Von Moltke was a man in his thirties who belonged to one of Germany's most famous noble families. The other leaders of the 'Kreisau Circle' were men of the same sort of age and background. Von Moltke and his friends were thinkers rather than men of action. They dreamed of a Germany without Hitler but rejected the idea of trying to overthrow him by force. The leaders of the 'Kreisau Circle' were rounded up and executed by the Nazis in 1944-5.

The leaders of the 'Beck-Goerdeler group' were men of an older generation than the members of the 'Kreisau Circle'. Ludwig Beck, a former army chief, was in his sixties and Karl Goerdeler, at one time Hitler's prices controller, was over 50. The 'Beck-Goerdeler group' was also more conservative in politics than the 'Kreisau Circle'. Von Moltke believed in democracy and a mild form of socialism. Goerdeler despised socialism and wanted to bring back the monarchy.

The biggest difference between the 'Kreisau Circle' and the 'Beck-Goerdeler group' concerned the use of violence. Beck and Goerdeler realised that the only way to get rid of Hitler was to kill him. They thought they could succeed. They had many supporters in the German army and so knew that they could get close to Hitler. The nearest they got to killing him was in July 1944. Claus von Stauffenberg, a senior army officer, was able to plant a bomb under the table in a conference-room used by Hitler. Four people were killed when it went off but Hitler escaped serious injury. Those connected with the 'July Plot' were executed.

Hitler surveys the damage done by the bomb attempt on his life.

Questions

1. Write a sentence to explain the role of each of the following in the resistance to Nazism: the Red Orchestra; Sophie Scholl; Helmuth von Moltke; Karl Goerdeler; Claus von Stauffenberg.
2. What incidents which took place during the late 1930s and early 1940s may have helped to convince people like von Moltke and Beck that Nazi rule was unacceptably brutal? (Refer to Units 3.1, 3.2 and 3.9 for ideas.)
3. Explain in your own words the difference between the methods of the 'Kreisau Circle' and those of the 'Beck-Goerdeler group'.
4. Can you suggest reasons why those who resisted Nazi rule never came together to form a united body?

Hitler's Foreign Policy Aims

Key ideas
1. Hitler aimed to create a 'Greater Germany'.
2. In addition Hitler aimed to win control of large parts of eastern Europe and the Soviet Union.

Core skills
1. Knowledge and understanding of Hitler's foreign policy aims.
2. Analysis of Hitler's foreign policy aims making use of the concepts of continuity and change.

Greater Germany

Hitler had two aims in foreign policy. One was to create a 'Greater Germany'. The other was to carve out a vast German Empire in eastern Europe.

The terms 'greater Germany' (Grossdeutschland) and 'little Germany' (Kleindeutschland) came into use in the nineteenth century. 'Greater Germany' was the term used to describe a Germany which contained all of the German-speaking people of Europe. 'Little Germany' was the term used to describe a Germany which contained only some of the German-speaking people of Europe.

There were two things that Hitler had to do if he was to succeed in his aim of creating a 'greater Germany'. One was to win back German-speaking areas such as Danzig and the Polish corridor which had been lost under the treaty of Versailles. The second thing was to win control of Austria and the area on Czechoslovakia's western border known as the Sudetenland. These were German-speaking areas which had not been part of pre-war Germany. The German Empire which had existed between 1871 and 1918 had been a 'little Germany'.

▶ What did Hitler mean by 'the right of national self-determination'? (go back to page 17 for ideas).

▶ Which European countries, other than Poland, Czechoslovakia and Austria, had reason to be alarmed by Hitler's plan for a 'Greater Germany'?

SOURCE 137 — Point One of the Nazi programme, 1920
We demand the union of all Germans in a Greater Germany on the basis of the right of national self-determination.
(J. Noakes and G. Pridham, 'Nazism 1919-45, vol 2', Exeter University Press, 1984)

SOURCE 138 — 'People of German Nationality' ('Das Deutschtum'); map from a 1930s German school atlas

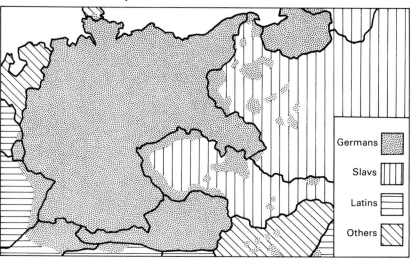

Germans

Slavs

Latins

Others

SOURCE 139 — Gottfried Feder, leading Nazi, writing in 1927

All those of German blood, even if they live at present under Danish, Polish, Italian or French sovereignty, are to be united in one German Reich . . .

(G. Feder, 'The Nazi Programme', Franz Eher Verlag, 1927)

The Nazis were not the first Germans to call for the creation of a 'greater Germany'. Before 1914 extreme German nationalists known as 'Pan-Germans' had done so. The German government, though, had made no move to meet their demands.

The Colonisation of Eastern Europe

In 'Mein Kampf' Hitler spoke of Germany's need for 'lebensraum' (living space). His demand for more living space was based on his belief that Germany was overcrowded.

SOURCE 140 — Hitler, writing in 1924

Germany has an annual increase in population of nearly nine hundred thousand souls. The difficulty of feeding this army of new citizens must grow greater . . . and ultimately end in catastrophe, unless ways and means are found to forestall the danger of starvation and misery in time.

(ed. J. Remak, 'The Nazi Years: A Documentary History', Prentice-Hall Inc.)

Hitler could have tried to get living space in the form of overseas colonies. This would have meant a return to the Kaiser's policies. Before 1914 the Kaiser had hoped to build a great German empire overseas. Hitler, though, was not greatly interested in overseas colonies. He seems to have felt that tropical areas were not suited to German settlement. He aimed instead at expansion in eastern Europe.

SOURCE 141 — Hitler, writing in 1924

We National Socialists consciously put an end to the foreign policy of our pre-war period. We . . . cast our eyes to the land in the East. We finally halt the colonial . . . policies of the pre-war period, and move on to the soil policy of the future. If we speak of soil in Europe today, we can think primarily only of Russia and the subject states bordering it.

(ed. J. Remak, 'The Nazi Years: A Documentary History', Prentice-Hall Inc.)

Hitler did not only want to win control of eastern Europe so that millions of Germans could be settled there. He also wanted to get his hands on its raw materials and agricultural produce. These were to be used to make Germany economically self-sufficient.

▶ What can we learn from this cartoon about Hitler's foreign policy aims?

SOURCE 142 — 'Come on, Joe (Stalin), those trousers will fit me fine. . .' (Daily Herald, 20 June 1941)

The Nazis did not see anything wrong in planning to take land from Russia. This was the result of their racism. The Nazis saw Russians as members of an inferior race. They did not even regard the Russians as full human beings. They saw them instead as 'Untermenschen' (sub-human).

SOURCE 143 — Robert Ley, speaking in 1939

The German race has higher rights than others. We have the divine right to rule and we shall assure ourselves of that right.

(quoted in W. Ebstein, 'The Nazi State', Octagon Books, 1943)

Questions

1. Write a sentence to explain the meaning of each of the following: Kleindeutschland; Pan-Germans; lebensraum.

2. Can you suggest one way in which Hitler's policy ideas resembled those of Kaiser William II?

3. In what way did Hitler's foreign policy ideas involve a departure from the foreign policy followed under Kaiser William II?

4. Did Hitler's ideas on foreign policy involve a complete change from the foreign policy which Stresemann had pursued, or did the two men have anything in common? (Go back to Unit 1.7 for information on Stresemann's foreign policy.)

German Expansion Before 1939

Key ideas

1. Between 1933 and 1939 Britain and France 'appeased' Hitler.
2. Between 1936 and 1939 Hitler reoccupied the Rhineland and won control of Austria and the Sudetenland without war.
3. In 1939 Hitler made a non-aggression pact with the Soviet Union.

Core skills

1. Knowledge and understanding of German expansion before 1939.
2. Analysis of the motives for the 'appeasement' policy followed by Britain and France before 1939.

In his early years in power Hitler was for the most part cautious in foreign affairs. He confined himself to gestures like withdrawing Germany from the League of Nations. He knew that Germany had to rearm before it could risk a clash with one of the big powers.

There was one occasion in these early years when Hitler was not cautious. In 1934 he got Nazi sympathisers in Austria to make a bid to bring about the Anschluss — the union of Austria and Germany. Italy stepped in and forced Hitler to give up his scheme. The Italians feared that a German-controlled Austria on their borders would mean trouble in their German-speaking province of South Tyrol.

In the mid-1930s Hitler was ready to embark on a more adventurous course. His main problem was the possibility that the other big powers in Europe would band together to try to stop him. Each of them had reason to fear him. He had made plain his intentions towards Russia. France dreaded that she would once again become a victim of German aggression. Britain did not want to see western Europe under the control of a single power that could close the continent to British trade. Italy was wary of Germany after the events of 1934.

When German rearmament was announced in 1935 Italy joined France and Britain in making a protest. Together the three countries formed what was called the 'Stresa Front'.

The big powers in Europe failed to stand together against Hitler. Italy made friends with Germany in 1936 and the 'Stresa Front' broke up. Britain decided on a policy of 'appeasing' Germany. 'Appeasement' involved trying to make agreements with Germany rather than standing up to her. France went along with Britain. Russia was left on her own. Russia and France did agree in 1935 to help each other in the event of a German attack on one of them but neither side seems to have taken the agreement very seriously.

SOURCE 144 — Baldwin, British Prime Minister, speaking in 1936

We all know the German desire as he [Hitler] has come out with it in his book, to move East; and if he moves East, I shall not break my heart . . . If there is any fighting in Europe to be done, I should like to see the Bolsheviks and the Nazis doing it.

(K. Middlemas and J. Barnes, 'Baldwin: a biography', Weidenfeld & Nicholson, 1969)

▶ What can you learn from these sources about the reasons why Britain pursued a policy of 'appeasement'?

SOURCE 145 — Frances Williams, British journalist, writing in 1939

The foreign policy of the British Government has been based on the idea that . . . Germany was anxious only for the settlement of claims which she rightly or wrongly felt to be justified. The Government believed, no doubt sincerely, that if Germany were assured that just claims could be satisfied by peaceful means, she would abandon her policy of aggression . . . Britain must now create the strongest conceivable system of defence, particularly against air attack. Upon the world's horror of aerial bombardment, the most loathsome of all the weapons in the modern armoury of war, Herr Hitler has founded his diplomacy.
('Daily Herald', 17 March 1939)

SOURCE 146 — Malcolm Macdonald, British MP, speaking in 1938

We are not strong enough to risk a war. It would mean the massacre of women and children on the streets of London.
(Harold Nicolson, 'Diaries and Letters 1930-39', Collins, 1971)

The willingness of Britain and France to appease Germany suited Hitler very well. Between 1936 and 1939 he got a long way towards creating a 'Greater Germany' without having to wage war.

The Reoccupation of the Rhineland, 1936

In March 1936 Hitler, without warning, sent German troops into the Rhineland. Under the Versailles treaty Germany was not allowed to station troops in the Rhineland.

SOURCE 147 — Lord Lothian, British politician, March 1936

The Germans . . . are only going into their own back garden.
(quoted in William L. Shirer, 'Rise and Fall of the Third Reich', Secker & Warburg, 1960)

SOURCE 148 — Harold Nicolson, British MP, March 1936

House [of Commons] crowded. Eden [Foreign Secretary] makes his statement . . . Promises to help France if attacked, otherwise negotiation. General mood of the House is one of fear. Anything to keep out of war.
(Harold Nicolson, 'Diaries and Leters 1930-39', Collins, 1971)

▶ Britain delivered a protest when the Rhineland was remilitarised. Why did she do nothing more?

The Anschluss, 1938

When Italy and Germany became friends the main obstacle to the Anschluss was removed. Austria soon came under threat. In 1938 Hitler called for Arthur Seyss-Inquart's Austrian Nazi party to be given a share in the government of Austria. Schuschnigg, Austria's Chancellor, refused to hand his country over to the Nazis. He arranged for a plebiscite to be held. His idea was to show that Austrians did not want the Anschluss. Hitler was furious. He threatened to invade Austria unless the plebiscite was called off and Schuschnigg resigned. The Austrians gave in. Seyss-Inquart was appointed Chancellor. He promptly invited German troops into Austria.

SOURCE 149 — Hitler, speaking in March 1938

What harm have we done to any foreign country? Whose interests have we hurt by falling in with the will of the overwhelming majority of the Austrian people to become Germans? I cannot understand the Anglo-French note of protest. These people are Germans.
(N. Baynes, 'Speeches of Adolf Hitler, vol II', Oxford University Press, 1942)

▶ What action did Britain and France take over the Anschluss?

▶ How did Hitler justify the Anschluss?

Munich, 1938

Hitler's next target was Czechoslovakia. His plan was to use the three million German-speaking people living in the Sudetenland to get what he wanted.

SOURCE 150 — The Sudetenland

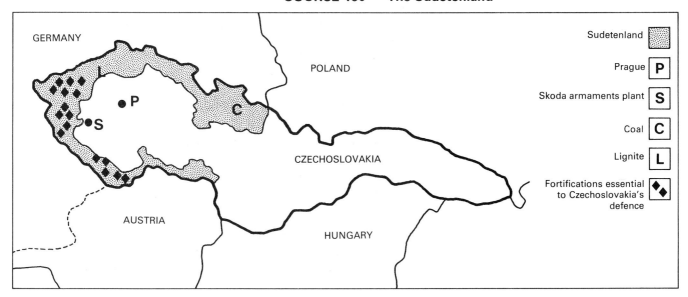

Legend:
- Sudetenland
- Prague — P
- Skoda armaments plant — S
- Coal — C
- Lignite — L
- Fortifications essential to Czechoslovakia's defence ◆

(Map labels: GERMANY, POLAND, CZECHOSLOVAKIA, AUSTRIA, HUNGARY)

▶ Suggest reasons why Czechoslovakia was anxious to retain control of the Sudentland.

There was in the Sudetenland a sizeable Nazi party led by Konrad Henlein. Hitler told Henlein in 1938 to demand all kinds of special treatment for the Sudeten Germans from the Czech government. He then hinted that Germany would go to war for the Sudeten Germans if their demands were not met.

The Czechs were by no means defenceless in the face of Hitler's threats. Czechoslovakia had modern industries and a well-equipped, though small, army. She also had powerful allies in the shape of France and Russia. Czechoslovakia's position was not, however, as strong as it appeared. Russia would not fight without France and France would not fight without Britain. Britain was unwilling to fight.

In September 1938 Chamberlain, Britain's prime minister, showed just how desperate he was to avoid war. He met Hitler at Berchtesgaden and agreed that those parts of the Sudetenland which were over 50 per cent German should be given to Germany. He then went away and got France and the Czechs to agree to this. He returned to Germany only to find that Hitler had changed his mind and was now demanding all of the Sudetenland. At this point war seemed close. The Italians then suggested a third meeting. Chamberlain and Daladier, the French prime minister, met Hitler at Munich and agreed to let him have what he wanted. The Czechs, deserted by their friends, had to give in.

The men of Munich: Chamberlain, Daladier, Hitler and Mussolini (from left to right)

The Destruction of Czechoslovakia, 1939

After Munich Hitler said that he had no more territorial demands to make in Europe. In March 1939 German troops marched into what was left of Czechoslovakia. The territory they occupied contained practically no German-speaking people.

▶ Why did the destruction of Czechoslovakia lead Britain to abandon the policy of 'appeasement'?

SOURCE 151 — Earl de la Warr, British Cabinet member, March 1939

This action of the Nazi regime has torn to shreds the last semblance of an excuse for their policy. Hitherto there has always been some attempt to justify their actions in terms either of the reincorporation of those of German race or of destroying some part of the Versailles treaty they have felt unjust. But today this veil . . . is no longer deemed necessary and aggression stands forth, naked and arrogant . . .

(quoted in the 'Daily Herald', 17 March 1939)

SOURCE 152 — 'The Glutton', Daily Herald, 17 March 1939

THE GLUTTON
The glutton is a deep water fish with an elastic stomach, which enables it to swallow an indefinite amount of prey.

▶ What view does the cartoonist take of the policy of 'appeasement'?

Poland, 1939

Britain guessed — correctly — that after Czechoslovakia Hitler would turn his attention to Poland. In March 1939 Poland was promised British help in the event of a German attack. This guarantee to Poland marked the end of 'appeasement'.

Britain's promise to Poland was to some extent an empty one. There was no possibility of British forces being able to get to Poland to fight. Britain therefore opened talks with Poland's neighbour, Russia. The purpose of the talks was to discuss the idea of an Anglo-Russian alliance to defend Poland. The talks failed. One reason for this was that Britain and Russia did not really trust each other. Another was that the Poles hated the Russians and did not want their help.

Germany also had talks with Russia in the summer of 1939. After the Polish guarantee Hitler knew that he would have to go to war to get Poland. He wanted to make sure that Poland was friendless and helpless when he attacked. Germany's talks with Russia were successful. The two countries made an agreement under which they promised not to go to war against each other. The agreement became known as the Nazi-Soviet non-aggression pact. The pact contained a secret clause under which Germany and Russia agreed to divide Poland between them. Germany attacked Poland a few days after the signing of the pact with Russia.

SOURCE 153 — German gains, 1933-39

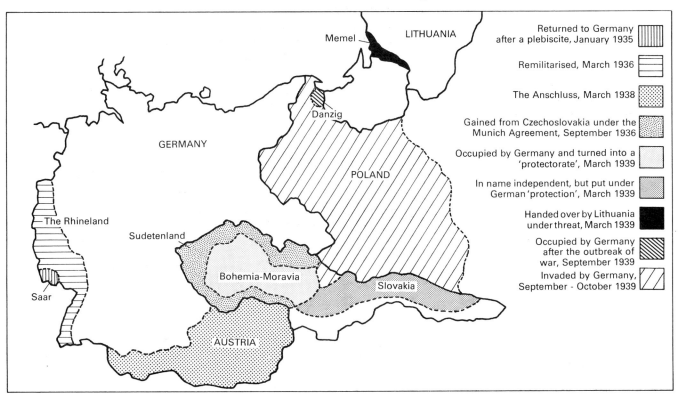

▶ Identify the gains made by Germany
before the outbreak of war which are not
referred to in the text.

Questions

1. Construct a time chart showing the gains of
   territory made by Nazi Germany between 1936
   and September 1939.
2. The Munich agreement was popular with British
   public opinion at the time that it was signed but
   the men who were responsible for it were heavily
   criticised. Can you account for
   i.   the popularity of the Munich agreement in
        Britain in 1938, and
   ii. its unpopularity later?
3. What is the difference between an alliance and a
   non-aggression pact? (see page 98 for help with
   what an alliance is).

4. Explain in your own words why Hitler made a
   non-aggression pact with the Soviet Union.
5. The general reaction in Europe to news of the
   Nazi-Soviet pact was one of surprise and
   astonishment: can you explain why this was so?
   (see pages 35, 43 and 91-2 for ideas).
6. 'Our enemies are small fry' (Hitler, speaking in
   September 1939). What evidence is there in the
   sources in this Unit which helps to explain why
   Hitler had such contempt for his enemies?

Hitler and His Allies

Key ideas

1. Germany and Italy were bound together by the Rome-Berlin Axis and later by the Pact of Steel and the Tripartite Axis.
2. Germany and Japan were linked by the Anti-Comintern Pact and later by the Tripartite Axis.

Core skills

1. Knowledge and understanding of Nazi Germany's friendships and alliances.
2. Analysis of Nazi Germany's friendships and alliances making use of the concepts of similarity and difference.

In 1933 Hitler's Germany was not on close terms with any of the world's big powers. By 1936 Hitler had established friendships with Italy and Japan. These friendships were later converted into alliances. When states make an alliance, they agree to help each other in time of war.

During the 1920s Hitler was an open admirer of Mussolini, Italy's fascist dictator. He also described Italy in 'Mein Kampf' as a possible ally for Germany. In private, though, he referred to the Italians in unflattering terms.

SOURCE 154 — Hitler on Italy, 1934

The Italians can never be trained to become a warlike people . . . Of course we can make temporary alliances with Italy; but ultimately we National Socialists stand alone.
(H. Rauschning, 'Hitler Speaks', Thornton Butterworth, 1939)

Mussolini's feelings about Hitler's arrival in power were mixed. He was to some extent pleased by the success of Nazism because he saw it as a creed which had much in common with his own. Italian fascists and German Nazis were alike in their hatred of communism and their contempt for democracy. There were, however, some differences of view.

▶ What differences were there between the views of Hitler and Mussolini on race and anti-semitism?

SOURCE 155 — Mussolini on race and anti-semitism, 1932

Of course there are no pure races left: not even the Jews have kept their blood unmingled. Successful crossings have often promoted the energy and the beauty of a nation . . . Anti-semitism does not exist in Italy. Italians of Jewish birth have shown themselves good citizens, and they fought bravely in the war.
(E. Ludwig, 'Talks with Mussolini', Little Brown, 1933)

'Two peoples and one struggle': German stamp, showing Hitler and Mussolini, 1941.

The main thing which kept Italy and Germany apart in the early 1930s was Hitler's designs on Austria. Mussolini's worries about the Anschluss were serious enough for him to join Britain and France in the 1935 'Stresa Front'. In 1936, though, he changed sides. He made an agreement with Hitler called the 'Rome-Berlin Axis'. Under this agreement Italy and Germany promised to work together in foreign affairs. One reason for Mussolini's about-turn was his quarrel with Britain and France over Italy's invasion of

Abyssinia (1935-6). Events in Spain were also important. The Spanish civil war (1936-9) was widely seen at the time as a kind of dress rehearsal for a bigger clash between communism and fascism. Hitler and Mussolini both sent troops to aid General Franco, the right-wing leader of the rebellion against Spain's left-wing government. The war convinced Mussolini of the need for partnership between the fascist powers.

In 1939 Germany and Italy made a full-scale alliance. It was known as the 'Pact of Steel'. It proved to be of little value to Germany. Italy entered the war late (1940) and collapsed in 1943.

Germany and Japan came together in 1936 when they signed the 'Anti-Comintern Pact'. On the surface the pact was just a vague agreement to resist the spread of communism by exchanging information about Comintern, the body through which Russia controlled the activities of the world's communist parties. Other countries were invited to join the pact, and some did — notably Italy (1937). Germany and Japan, however, had more in common than anti-communism. Both wanted to weaken Russia. In Japan's case this was because she felt that Russia stood in the way of her plans to colonise China. The 1936 pact included a secret arrangement for co-operation against Russia. The Germany-Japan link was seen in other countries as a surprising one.

SOURCE 156 — H-J Koehler, Nazi sympathiser, on the race issue, 1940

Hitler and Rosenberg maintain that the German race is chosen by destiny to rule the world because it is superior to all other races. In subtle grading the rest of the world follows . . . The yellow races are near the bottom.

(H. J. Koehler, 'Inside Information', Pallas Publishing, 1940)

SOURCE 157 — Daily Herald, 27 November 1936

(The cartoon was prompted by the Anti-Comintern Pact. Note that Franco used African troops in the Spanish Civil War.)

EUROPEAN CONCERT
" . . in the service of European culture and civilisation."
—Nazi Press Chief on the Tokyo Pact.

▶ What message do you think the cartoonist is trying to put across?

▶ How might a cartoonist hostile to Nazism have drawn attention to the differences between Germany and Italy at the time the Rome-Berlin Axis was formed?

Once the pact with Japan had been made Nazi leaders, at least in public, found much to praise in Japan society.

SOURCE 158 — Alfred Rosenberg, leading Nazi, on Japan, 1938
The 2000 year-old Japanese state appears to us admirable for its religious unity, state discipline, and stamp of national sacrifice.
(quoted in E. L. Priessen, 'Germany and Japan', Howard Fertig, 1969)

Relations between Germany and Japan went sour when the Nazi-Soviet pact was signed in 1939. Things improved when Germany attacked Russia in 1941. Japan joined Germany and Italy in an alliance called the 'Tripartite Axis'. It was not a close alliance. What Germany and Japan looked forward to was a world in which each was supreme in its own area — Germany in Europe, Japan in Asia.

Questions
1. Explain in your own words
   i. why Mussolini lined up against Hitler before 1935
   ii. why Mussolini decided to make an agreement with Hitler in 1936.
2. Make as full a list as you can of the similarities between Fascist Italy and Nazi Germany.
3. Make as full a list as you can of the things that Germany and Japan had in common in the 1930s.

4. How do you think Japan reacted to news of the Nazi-Soviet Pact in 1939?
5. 'Nazi Germany's link with Japan was more surprising than her link with Mussolini's Italy'. Do you agree with this opinion? Give reasons for your answer.

Germany at War

Key ideas

1. Germany's armies scored spectacular successes, 1939-41.
2. After 1943 Germany was on the retreat.
3. During the last years of the war German towns and cities were very heavily bombed.

Core skills

1. Knowledge of Nazi Germany's main victories and defeats, 1939-45.
2. Empathetic understanding of the attitudes of Germany's civilian population during the war years.

In 1939 Germany crushed Poland in a few weeks. The Polish campaign was followed by a six-month period in which little fighting took place. This period came to an end when Hitler occupied Norway and Denmark in April 1940. His aim was to safeguard the iron ore which was exported from Sweden to Germany through Norway. The fall of Norway was quickly followed by the fall of Holland, Belgium and France (May-June 1940). Next came the Luftwaffe's bid to win control of the skies over Britain. The bid failed. German plans for the invasion of Britain were shelved. Hitler's thoughts turned to Russia. He prepared the ground for an attack on Russia by tightening his grip on south-eastern Europe. Hungary, Rumania and Bulgaria were forced to become Germany's allies (August 1940-February 1941). Yugoslavia and Greece were invaded (April 1941). The attack on Russia ('Operation Barbarossa') was launched in June 1941. A huge area of western Russia fell to the Nazis in the first year of fighting. In early 1942 Hitler was at the height of his power.

Hitler's early successes were based on a style of warfare known as 'blitzkrieg' ('lightning war'). Planes and tanks were used in combination to punch holes in the enemy's defences: the infantry poured through the gaps that were created.

Hitler's Empire, 1942

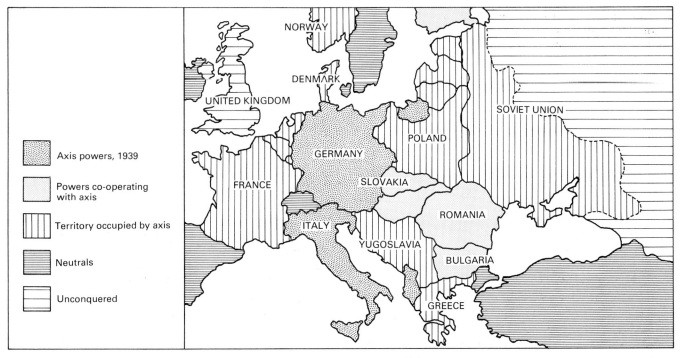

Axis powers, 1939

Powers co-operating with axis

Territory occupied by axis

Neutrals

Unconquered

Soviet stamp issued on the 20th anniversary of the Battle of Kursk

In December 1941 Hitler declared war on the United States following the Japanese attack on Pearl Harbour. This was a fatal decision. The American economy was the most powerful in the world. The strength of the United States soon began to tell. In 1943 Anglo-American forces crossed to Italy after defeating the Germans in North Africa. In June 1944 an Anglo-American army under Eisenhower landed in northern France.

By this time the Germans had been forced out of Russia. Their retreat followed defeat in two crucial battles in 1942-3. One was the six-month battle for Stalingrad in which nearly 300,000 Germans were either killed or taken prisoner. The other was the battle of Kursk (July 1943). Kursk was the greatest tank battle the world has seen.

Hitler hoped in 1939 that he could win the war without imposing heavy strains on Germany's civilian population. He was frightened of popular discontent. In the first years of the war, therefore, there were still goods in German shops and food rationing was not too severe. Things changed when Germany's armies got bogged down in Russia. Hitler accepted that strict control of Germany's resources could not be avoided. In 1942 he made Albert Speer Armaments Minister. Speer's task was to organise the country for 'total war'. It was at just the point that economic life was put under stricter control that Germany began to experience heavy British and American bombing raids. Between 1942 and 1945 German cities were bombed remorselessly.

▶ How would you describe the reactions of ordinary Germans to the experience of being bombed?

▶ Do you find these reactions surprising or unsurprising?

▶ Do you think those in charge of the Allied bombing campaign would have been pleased or disappointed to learn of these reactions?

SOURCE 159 — Marie Vassiltchikov, Berliner, 1943

The Allied advance in Italy is not proceeding very fast. It looks as if these ghastly raids are intended to help their progress by breaking the Germans' morale, but I do not think that much can be achieved that way. Indeed they are having the contrary effect. For amid such suffering and hardship, political considerations become secondary and everyone seems intent only on patching roofs, propping up walls . . . or melting snow for water to wash with. Furthermore, at such times the heroic side of human nature takes over and people are being extraordinarily friendly and helpful to one another.
(M. Vassiltchikov, 'The Berlin Diaries, 1940-45', Chatto & Windus, 1985)

SOURCE 160 — Christabel Bielenberg, 1943

I learned when I was in Berlin that those wanton, quite impersonal killings, that barrage from the air which mutilated, suffocated burned and destroyed, did not so much breed fear and a desire to bow before the storm, but rather a certain fatalistic cussedness, a dogged determination to survive and if, possible, help others to survive, whatever their politics, whatever their creed.
(Christabel Bielenberg. 'The Past is Myself', Chatto & Windus, 1968)

SOURCE 161 — Mathilde Wolff-Monckeberg, Hamburg housewife, 1943

People here are curiously apathetic and dull. On their faces one can read despair, can sense wretchedness, irritation and exasperation wherever one happens to be: on the tram, in the post office, in the shops. How different the atmosphere is from the first war year, when at the slightest provocation red Nazi flags were flown, drums were beaten on the radio announcing victory, and everyone

bragged outrageously. Since the capitulation of Stalingrad and the realisation of total war, all is grey and still. Shop after shop has closed down, one tolerates discomforts, forgets that life was ever different . . .
(M. Wolff-Monckeberg, 'On The Other Side', Peter Owen Ltd, 1979)

An air raid on Berlin, 1943. The mother is wearing a gas mask and has wrapped herself and the pram in wet blankets for protection against fire and smoke.

SOURCE 162 — Hamburg housewife, 1944

Our people have limitless patience and perseverance. Our butter ration has just been cut again, three instead of four issues per month, but the only reaction is quiet grumbles and sighs. 'Can you manage?' one asks the other. 'Got to,' is the typical reply . . .
(M. Wolff-Monckeberg, 'On The Other Side', Peter Owen Ltd, 1979)

SOURCE 163 — 'Defence of the Nazi Home Front'; cartoon by David Low, August 1943

BE CAREFUL TO FIX THEM SO THAT THEY CAN TURN BOTH WAYS

▶ How do Source 163 and Source 164 differ in their view of the attitude of ordinary Germans to the Nazis in the later stages of the war?

▶ Which of them do you think was the most accurate?

SOURCE 164 — British Intelligence report on German morale, 1944

The German masses are so fatalistic, so weary, so lacking in initiative and so terrified of Nazi repression as to be incapable of supporting or indeed of taking very much interest in an attempt to overthrow the regime.

(quoted in M. Balfour, 'Propaganda In War 1939-45', Routledge & Kegan Paul, 1979)

Questions

1. Put the following events into the correct chronological sequence:
    a. the start of Operation Barbarossa,
    b. the German invasion of France,
    c. Hitler's declaration of war on the United States,
    d. the battle of Stalingrad,
    e. the battle of Kursk.
2. Which of the countries which fought against Hitler would you say was mainly responsible for his defeat? Give reasons for your answer.
3. Study Source 161. What seems to have been the mood of the German people during the early years of the war?
4. Study Sources 160, 161 and 164. How did the mood of the German people change as the war went on?
5. How would you account for the changing mood of the German people during the course of the war?

After Hitler: Germany 1945-1949

Key ideas

1. Nazi leaders who survived the war were put on trial as war criminals at Nuremberg.
2. The Allies agreed that Germany should be split into four zones of occupation until such time as the terms of a final peace treaty were decided.
3. Quarrels among the Allies led in 1949 to the creation of the Federal Republic of Germany and the German Democratic Republic.

Core skills

1. Knowledge and understanding of the occupation arrangements for Germany made by the Allies.
2. Knowledge and understanding of the reasons why the Federal Republic of Germany and the German Democratic Republic were created in 1949.

The Russian flag raised over the Reichstag, 1945

Hitler spent the last months of his life in a bunker beneath the Reich Chancellery in Berlin. By this time his enemies were closing in around him. In January 1945 the Russian army crossed from Poland into eastern Germany. Two months later British and American forces began to invade Germany from the west. In April 1945 the Russians reached the outskirts of Berlin.

Hitler killed himself on 30 April. Goebbels and Himmler died in the same way. Goebbels committed suicide in Berlin the day after Hitler. Himmler tried to avoid capture by disguising himself as an ordinary soldier but killed himself when he was found out.

Twenty-one leading Nazis were put on trial for war crimes at Nuremberg in 1945-6. Eleven were hanged. Others, among them Speer, were given long prison sentences. The most important defendant at Nuremberg was Goering. He was sentenced to death but committed suicide before the sentence could be carried out.

In May 1945 Germany surrendered unconditionally to her enemies. The Allies — Russia, Britain and the United States — now had to decide what was to be done with Germany. They made their arrangements at two 'summit' conferences in 1945. One was held in February at Yalta in southern Russia. Present at Yalta were Roosevelt (USA), Churchill (Britain) and Stalin (Russia). The second conference took place at Potsdam, near Berlin, in August. There were some new faces at Potsdam. Truman had replaced Roosevelt as US President and Attlee had taken over from Churchill as British Prime Minister.

The Potsdam conference: East German 25th anniversary stamp

Three main decisions affecting Germany were reached at Yalta and Potsdam. These were the decisions about the Polish border, about zones of occupation and about the policies which were to be followed in the occupation zones.

Germany's Border with Poland

In 1945 changes were made in Germany's border with Poland. These changes arose out of Russia's demand for eastern Poland. This was a region which had belonged to Russia before it was taken by Poland in 1920. Russia had got it back in 1939 and in 1945 was determined to keep it. The Russians said that Poland could be given part of Germany as compensation for her losses. Britain and the United States went along with this idea. The new German-Polish border followed the course of the rivers Oder and Neisse. It became known as the 'Oder-Neisse line'.

Zones of Occupation

Germany and Austria were divided into four occupation zones in 1945. Special arrangements were made for Berlin. Each of the four occupying powers was given a sector of Berlin to administer. Russia promised to allow the other three powers access to their sectors from their occupation zones in western Germany.

It was not the intention of the Allies to occupy Germany forever. Their plan was for the occupation to continue until they decided that Germans were fit to govern themselves again. At this point there was to be final peace treaty between Germany and the Allies.

Border changes and occupation zones, 1945

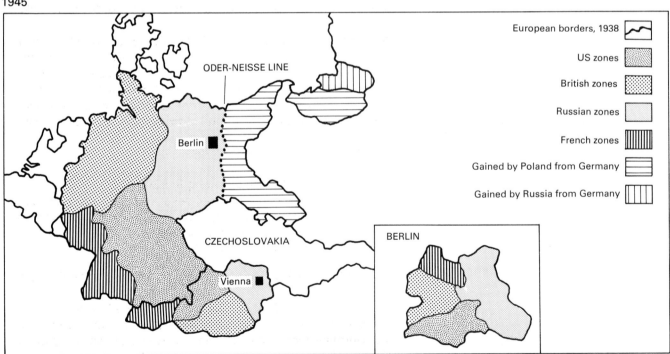

Governing the Occupation Zones

The occupying powers did not get the right in 1945 to do as they liked in their own zones. What they devised was a system of joint control. An Allied Control Council (ACC) was set up to work out policies which were to be applied in each of the zones. The ACC was made up of the commanders of the four zones. The commanders were to be guided by general principles agreed among the Allies.

SOURCE 165 — Agreement made at Potsdam, 1945

The purposes of the occupation of Germany by which the Control Council shall be guided are:

The complete disarmament and demilitarisation of Germany . . .

To destroy the National Socialist Party . . . to dissolve all Nazi institutions, to ensure that they are not revived in any form, and to prevent all Nazi and militarist activity or propaganda . . .

To prepare for the eventual reconstruction of German political life on a democratic basis and for eventual peaceful co-operation in international life by Germany . . .

The administration of affairs in Germany should be directed towards the decentralisation of the political structure and the development of local responsibility . . .

('Foreign Relations of the United States', 1945)

▶ Five words starting with 'd' can be used to sum up the aims that the occupying powers agreed in 1945 to pursue in Germany. One of them is 'denazification'. Can you suggest the other four?

The agreements made about Germany in 1945 soon began to break down. The wartime Allies quarrelled. There were disputes between Russia on the one hand and the USA and Britain on the other about Russia's takeover of eastern Europe. These disputes made it difficult for the powers to co-operate in Germany. Disputes also arose out of events which took place in Germany itself.

In the years between 1945 and 1948, Britain and the USA found it increasingly hard to contain their anger over what was happening in the Russian zone. The Russians, for their part, complained about developments in the western zones. These complaints became especially loud when Britain and the USA turned their zones into a single economic unit known as 'Bizonia' in 1947.

SOURCE 166 — Lucius Clay, US Military Governor in Germany

The Soviets . . . carried away by their first sight of modern German factories . . . believed that their way to economic progress lay in dismantling entire plants and factories in Germany for re-erection in Soviet Russia. They began this dismantling process early, and soon railroad cars were passing through Berlin laden down with equipment.

(Lucius Clay, 'Decision in Germany', Heinemann, 1950)

SOURCE 167 — Stalin, speaking in 1945

This war is not as in the past: whoever occupies a territory also imposes on it his own social system. Everyone imposes his own social system as far as his army has power to do so.

(M. Djilas, 'Conversations with Stalin', Rupert Hart Davis, 1962)

▶ What policies were pursued by the Russians in their zone after 1945 and why did these anger Britain and the United States?

SOURCE 168 — Karl Brandt, American writer, on the Russian zone

Seventeen million Germans are living under Red Army occupation. . . There is neither freedom of speech or of assembly. The Germans there live virtually in slavery in a ruthlessly exploited Soviet colony.

('Vital Speeches of the Day', November 1949)

SOURCE 169 — US Ambassador, Moscow, writing in 1947

War has left Russia with a deep awareness of the realities of German aggression. A determination to prevent the resurgence of a strong and independent and possibly hostile Germany is surely the major preoccupation of Soviet policy.

('Foreign Relations of the United States, 1947, vol II')

▶ What policies did Britain and the United States pursue in their zones and why did these cause alarm in Russia?

SOURCE 170 — Ernest Bevin, British Foreign Secretary, 1948

We have no desire to create a Germany which can ever be aggressive, but Germany cannot be allowed to remain a slum in the centre of Europe. Our policy is that she must contribute to her own recovery and keep herself . . . On the principle of political development we have come to the conclusion that we must give the Germans responsibility and the necessary authority.

(B. Ruhm von Oppen, 'Documents on Germany Under Occupation', Oxford University Press & the Royal Institute of International Affairs, 1955)

In June 1948 an important step towards unity was taken in the western zones. A new currency (the Deutschmark) was introduced in order to promote economic revival. The currency reform brought Allied disagreements over Germany to a head. The Russians claimed that the western zones were about to be turned into a separate country. They walked out of the ACC saying that joint control of Germany was at an end. Soon afterwards Russia started to prevent the free movement of land traffic in and out of Berlin. The Russians wanted to force the western powers out of the city and to gain full control over eastern Germany. They justified the 'Berlin blockade' by saying that they no longer had to obey the 1945 agreements because the western powers had broken them. The western response to the blockade was the Berlin airlift. For almost a year west Berlin's two million citizens were supplied from the air. The Russians called off the blockade in May 1949.

▶ In what ways does this cartoon help us to understand the Berlin airlift was a remarkable achievement?

SOURCE 171 — 'The Bird Watcher', Punch, British magazine, July 1946

When the airlift ended the western powers and the Russians made their own arrangements in their own zones. In September 1949 the western zones were put together to form a country named Federal Republic of Germany. The first leader of the Federal Republic was Konrad Adenauer. The Russian zone became the German Democratic Republic in October 1949. Its leader was Walther Ulbricht.

The division of Germany into two parts lasted for more than forty years. Until the late 1980s it appeared likely that the division would prove to be permanent. What changed things was the coming to power in the Soviet Union of Mikhail Gorbachev. It became clear that under Gorbachev the Soviet Union would not stand in the way of German reunification. East Germany became part of a united Germany in October 1990.

Questions

1. Put the following events into the correct chronological sequence:
   a. the creation of the German Democratic Republic,
   b. the establishment of Bizonia,
   c. the Potsdam conference,
   d. the creation of the Federal Republic of Germany,
   e. the unconditional surrender of Nazi Germany,
   f. the Yalta conference.

2. Write a sentence to explain what you understand by each of the following: summit conferences; the Oder-Neisse line; denazification; Bizonia.

3. Study Sources 166, 167 and 169. What motives do you think lay behind the policies followed by the Soviet Union in her zone of Germany?

4. Who do you think was mainly responsible for the breakdown of co-operation among the Allies in Germany — the Soviet Union or Britain and the United States? Give reasons for your answer.

Glossary

Anti-Semitism	hatred of Jews
Aristocracy	the nobility
Armistice	cease-fire
Autarky	economic self-sufficiency
Boycott	refusal to have dealings with someone
Capitalism	economic system based on private ownership and profit
Cession	to give up property
Chancellor	German prime minister
Coalition	government containing more than one party
Communists	extreme socialists — believers in the ideas of Karl Marx
Concordat	agreement between the Pope and a country's government
Constitution	the set of rules, usually contained in a single document, by which a state is governed
'Co-ordination'	process by which important organisations were brought under Nazi control
Demilitarised Zone	area in which no fortifications are built and no troops are stationed
'Diktat'	dictated peace
'Einsatzgruppen'	SS murder gangs
General Strike	a strike of all workers
Gestapo	Nazi secret police
Hyperinflation	very rapid fall in the value of money
Indoctrination	getting someone to believe completely in an idea
Junkers	Prussian landowners
Kaiser	the German emperor
'Kampfzeit'	'time of struggle' — term used by Nazis to describe 1919-33
Luftwaffe	the German air force
Mark	Germany's currency
Marxist	communist
Nationalist	someone who believed that Germany should be great and powerful
'November Criminals'	those responsible for the 1918 armistice
Passive Resistance	disobedience without violence
Plebiscite	vote of the people on an important question
President	German head of state
Proportional Representation	voting system in which parties win seats in relation to the percentage of the vote they win
Prussia	largest of the states which made up the German Empire and the Weimar Republic
Putsch	a bid to seize power by force
Racist	believer in the superiority of one race over another
Reparations	payments made by countries losing a war to the winners
Republican	supporter of the Weimar constitution
Reichstag	the German parliament
Ruhr	Germany's main industrial area
Self-Determination	the right of people to decide for themselves which state they want to belong to
Socialism	economic system built around public rather than private ownership
Summit Conferences	meetings between important heads of government
Totalitarian	one-party state in which rulers try to control totally the lives of the ruled
'Untermenschen'	sub-human

Index